Purchased at
The All England Lawn Tennis
and Croquet Club
Wimbledon, England
Tuesday, June 5, 1990

THE CHAMPIONSHIPS
WIMBLEDON

Official Annual 1989

JOHN PARSONS
Photographs by TOMMY HINDLEY

AURUM PRESS

Photographs copyright © Tommy Hindley 1989; additional
photographs by Michael Cole and also by Professional Sport
photographic team of Philip Shephard-Lewis, Jim Steele and
Richard Kelly. The photograph on p.5 is copyright © Sarah
Watson; on pp. 12–13 © Aerofilms Ltd; on p.111 (bottom)
© Russ Adams.

First published 1989 by Aurum Press Ltd,
33 Museum Street, London WC1A 1LD

British Library Cataloguing in Publication Data

The Championships Wimbledon: official annual.
   – 1989
   1. London. Merton. (London Borough). Lawn tennis.
   Competitions: Lawn Tennis Championships. Serials
   I. All England Lawn Tennis & Croquet Club
   796.342′09421′93

ISBN 1 85410 072 6

Designed by Philip Mann/Ace Ltd

Typeset by Spectrum Typesetting Ltd, London
Colour origination by Speedlith Group, Manchester
Printed in Great Britain by Butler and Tanner Ltd, Frome

FOREWORD

This is the seventh Official Wimbledon Annual, relating and recording the highlights of a remarkably interesting fortnight. What a pity the idea of an annual only started in 1983, and what a wonderful parade it would have made had this been the 103rd, stretching from 1877 to the present day.

Most people will agree that the two weeks in 1989 produced some great matches, even though there were seven days on which rain interrupted play. However, the speed in covering all 18 grass courts ensured that resumption was possible very shortly after the heavens relented. We aimed to have all the courts covered within two minutes, but in practice the average was more like one minute. Indeed, so quick and efficient were the strong men who pulled the Centre Court canvas across the court that the spectators actually applauded.

1989 will go down in history as the year when the young seemed to be taking over; when, sadly, Chrissie Evert may have played in her last Centre Court match; and when Steffi Graf and Boris Becker were the new champions – Steffi for the second year running and Boris for the third time in five years.

How astonishing that these two great champions should live within 10 miles of each other in West Germany. The new generation will surely be born, not so much with silver spoons as with tennis rackets in their mouths. There will be an even greater upsurge in the popularity of lawn tennis there from now on.

Inevitably, there have to be losers. Many of us were sad and sympathetic when Ivan Lendl did not achieve his greatest ambition and when both Stefan Edberg and Martina Navratilova fell at the last hurdle. The sheer power of Boris Becker and, indeed, of Steffi Graf was positively awesome, each of them worthy champions.

Now that the tumult and shouting – of which there was rather too much – have died down, I hope you will enjoy the photography of Tommy Hindley and the day-by-day descriptions of the matches by John Parsons. They say it all.

R.E.H.Hadingham, CBE, MC, TD

Chairman of The All England Club and the Committee of Management of The Lawn Tennis Championships.

July 1989

INTRODUCTION

The countdown to The Championships at Wimbledon in 1989 could not have been more intriguing. That was particularly so after the stunning events at the French Open a few weeks earlier, culminating in the emergence of two 17-year-olds as the champions, Michael Chang and Arantxa Sanchez Vicario.

Few genuinely expected either the delightful *señorita* from Spain, who had lost in the first round on both her previous visits to Wimbledon, or the Chinese-American, extraordinarily resilient, both mentally and physically for his age, to repeat their clay-court triumphs on grass. Yet they had stirred the pot excitingly at just the right time.

Their victories in Paris certainly broadened the horizons. Could Martina Navratilova, for instance, who had forsaken the clay-court tournaments completely to concentrate on grass-court preparation, now be inspired to reach even greater heights, in her passionate campaign for a record ninth title, by the thought that perhaps Steffi Graf might after all be vulnerable? Or would the West German, who had clearly not been at her best, physically, in Paris, simply be made even more determined than ever after her first defeat in six Grand Slam tournaments to restore and underline her dominance?

The seedings indicated continuing faith in the belief that world number one, Ivan Lendl, would

at last win the only Grand Slam tournament which continued to elude him. There was much sentimental support – not least from his fellow professionals – for the tall, angular, hard-hitting player who had worked so hard for more than a decade, since winning the junior boys' title. When, after his premature defeat in Paris, he became a late entry for The Stella Artois Championships at Queen's Club and won a senior grass-court tournament for the first time in his career, some felt it was a lucky omen.

Ready to destroy the Lendl dream, however, were, among others, three of the four players seeded immediately behind him, all of whom knew what it means to be Wimbledon champion and were convinced they were capable of becoming so again – defending champion Stefan Edberg and former champions Boris Becker and John McEnroe.

The bookmakers made Becker the favourite and there was the prospect, therefore, of a West German double for the first time in the history of The Championships. No one could reasonably dismiss the possibility of a repeat victory by Edberg, however, especially as his all-round game had been looking stronger and more mature than ever. As for McEnroe, who had also bypassed Paris so as not to distract his grass-court timing, he was convinced he was closer than at any time since 1984 to regaining his Championship peak.

One way and another, the 103rd staging of The Championships, 112 years after the first in 1877, promised to be as richly compelling as all those which had gone before. The pages which follow illustrate how magnificently, despite the weather, that promise was fulfilled.

All the photographs in this Official Wimbledon Annual were taken on 'Kodak' EKTACHROME Professional Film and KODACHROME Professional Film.

D A Y

1

Monday 26 June

Except perhaps for the finals, there is no time at Wimbledon which grips the imagination more than Day One. For many, competitors and spectators alike, it is akin to the dawning of a new year; certainly it is the moment in the tennis year that launches the period which means most to them.

It applies just as much to those who have walked or been driven through the Church Road gates for the first time as it does to Chris Evert and Jimmy Connors who, on their 18th visit, could hardly imagine a time in their lives when Wimbledon was not the pinnacle of their year's work.

Certainly there was a heady cross-section of such emotions experienced throughout the 18 courts on Day One of Wimbledon '89, as two of the most recent men's singles champions, Boris Becker and reigning title-holder Stefan Edberg, together with Ivan Lendl – still searching for elusive Wimbledon glory – and the remarkable Monica Seles – still almost an innocent child at play in a sternly adult world – provided The Championships with a flying start, and without a single umbrella in sight.

The Duchess of York, an avid tennis follower, was among a record first-day attendance of 34,154 who watched Edberg launch proceedings on Centre Court, as tradition demands. The Swede, who took only 75 seconds to swoop in behind

Jimmy Connors has seen it all before.

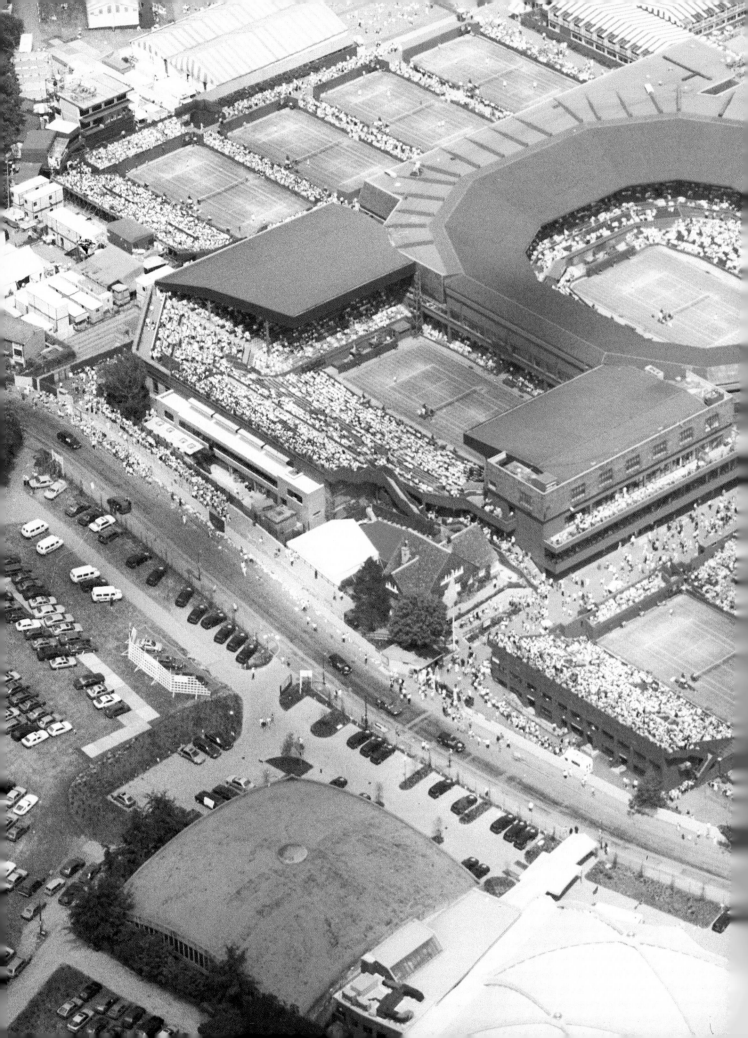

Few opening day problems for defending champion, Stefan Edberg (left).

Ivan Lendl was often kept at full stretch by Pereira.

four splendidly positive first serves in the first game, beat Canadian Chris Pridham, 6–3, 6–4, 6–1, in a style befitting his reputation.

'I didn't try anything fancy, I just played pretty solidly,' said Edberg, in his typically low-key approach. 'I don't think you can expect to play perfectly straight off in a tournament like this, although I went pretty close to it in the third set.'

Although there are more than 1,000 players ranked on the men's circuit, the tennis world is still small enough for most to know their own, or each other's, opponents pretty well. Three days before the draw, Edberg and Pridham had agreed to practise together, never dreaming that they might be facing each other in the opening Centre Court contest. Edberg also realized only too intensely how top-seeded Lendl was probably feeling as he walked out on Court 1 to face Nicolas Pereira, 18, from Venezuela, the world junior champion who had not only won the junior boy's singles title at Wimbledon in 1988, but in his most recent Grand Prix match had beaten Edberg on grass in The Stella Artois Championships at Queen's Club. Edberg, it is true, was at the time still suffering a hangover from his stunning defeat by Michael Chang in the French Open final on clay 48 hours earlier, but the match also offered more than a hint about Pereira's budding potential and explains why, at one stage, the spectre of a first-day defeat in The Championships hung over Lendl.

When Pereira took the fourth-set tie-break, historians were beginning to recall how Manuel Santana, in 1967, was the last top seed to lose in the first round. That, however, was the signal for Lendl to restore order. He almost immediately lifted his game to win 7–6, 4–6, 6–3, 6–7, 6–1 after 3 hours 15 minutes. However, the sturdily built teenager had more than a few moments of glory, not least when he took the second set with two consecutive aces, while the electric scoreboard at the Members' End, as if disbelieving the situation, remained stuck at 5–4.

Lendl, despite making short work of the final set, laboured heavily. With a touch more experience, Pereira's name might have been emblazoned across all the sports pages the following day, instead of simply being consigned to the 'one to watch for the future' file. It all started to go wrong for the occasionally over-exuberant teenager when he played what Lendl called 'a terrible game' to be broken in the sixth game of the third set. Although Lendl, who overall hit 20 aces, still lost the fourth set, he blamed himself for that.

Becker, meanwhile, hit 18 aces and 10 double faults as Court 2 held few terrors for him while he overcame Brian Shelton, a black American qualifier from Georgia Tech University, who was playing in a Grand Prix tournament for the first time.

After Edberg, Centre Court was occupied by what might be termed the old and the new worlds of tennis. First there was Connors, at 36 just as pugnacious as ever on court while beating the Russian, Andrei Cherkasov, 6–3, 6–2, 4–6, 6–3, and also later in the interview room while discussing his performance.

Then came Chang, 17, the young lion from Roland Garros, who kept the arena well filled until 8.28 pm as he beat Bill Scanlon – still keen enough at 32 and ten years after he was a quarter-finalist to battle his way through the qualifying rounds at Roehampton – 6–4, 6–3, 2–6, 6–3. Although Chang trailed 1–3 in the fourth set, there were again times when he unleashed those electrifying double-handed backhand passes which had won him a late-night ovation against Henri Leconte in the same setting a year earlier, and which first alerted so many to the richness of his promise.

Jakob Hlasek, finding it increasingly difficult to sustain his top-ten ranking and even more his sixth seeding, became the first seeding casualty in the men's singles when he was beaten 6–3, 7–6, 6–1 by Sweden's 119th-ranked Thomas Hogstedt. The score in the third set reflected the growing despair of a splendid ambassador for the game and for Switzerland, his adopted country. After losing in the fourth round at the French Open on his best surface, Hlasek had spent two weeks trying to become better acquainted with the surface he trusts the least.

Anne Minter, the elder of two Australian tennis-playing sisters, had the quickest win on the opening day. She beat Molly Van Nostrand of the United States 6–0, 6–0. But there was no

Nicolas Pereira (above right) made it a tough opening day for Ivan Lendl.

Bill Scanlon was impressed by his first close look at Michael Chang.

Tomas Hogstedt, from Sweden, on his way to becoming the first to beat a seed, Jakob Hlasek.

The scoreboard in the background shows how close Holland's Brenda Schultz came, at 4–2 in the final set, to beating Monica Seles.

doubt which competitor in the women's singles had the biggest following. That was Miss Seles, a prodigy since she first represented Yugoslavia at an international event in Florida at the age of nine and won the 12-and-under title. The grunt and the ferocious power in those double-handed groundstrokes were already there then, I remember. The giggle, another of her trademarks now, came later. Yet it was the strength of character under acute pressure for one so young which most intrigued, as well as impressed, not only the packed crowd round Court 2 but also many of her peers filling the players' balcony above. Miss Seles, who had gone so close to upsetting Steffi Graf in the semi-finals in Paris just

over a fortnight earlier, won the first competitive match of her life on grass, 7–6, 1–6, 6–4, against the 1988 junior champion, Brenda Schultz from Holland.

As she left she responded to the cheers with a customary wave and said, 'I liked it.' She quite clearly had done, even though she was honest enough to admit that when trailing 4–2 in the final set with the powerful Dutch girl holding a point for 5–2 she thought the match was 'getting away from me'.

It was in those next few games that Miss Seles demonstrated not only her best tennis but a champion's mentality. While Miss Schultz lapsed into costly errors, Miss Seles tightened her game,

Boris Becker hit 18 aces in a smooth first-round ride.

especially the serve, saving the second of two more arguably crucial break points at 4–4 with a resounding ace down the middle. Lewis Carroll would have enjoyed every minute.

As always on the opening day, there was much attention to British performances and with it much stretching of loyalties and emotions, not least on Court 14 where Jeremy Bates, who the year before had recovered from two sets down to beat Christo Van Rensburg, this time rallied from two sets to one down, plus a break down in the fourth, to overcome Brazil's Cassio Motta, 6–7, 6–1, 4–6, 7–6, 6–3. Depending on which bits of the match one happened to catch, on a day when it

was impossible to devote much time to any one in order to keep abreast of so much activity, you were either amazed that Bates survived or astonished that it took him so long to win.

The most encouraging first-day British victory was provided by Nick Fulwood, who had reacted in the best possible manner to the disappointment of not being given a wild card by winning through three qualifying rounds, to be in the draw on merit. He beat the American, Jonathan Canter, 7–6, 3–6, 7–6, 7–6 and emphasized his serving confidence by taking the three tie-breaks 7–1, 7–3 and then 7–2.

Fulwood's victory lined up a first meeting in

A parting of the ways for Nick Fulwood (above) and Roger Smith, after the British player won three tie-breaks against Jonathan Canter but Smith, the Bahamian, was beaten in the first round.

senior tennis for him against Mark Petchey, 19, from Essex who, despite being in bed with food poisoning the day before, had outplayed Fernando Luna of Spain, a clay-court specialist, 6–2, 6–7, 6–2, 6–1. Luna was ranked 73 in the world at the time; Petchey 313. Petchey's wild card had been justified.

Next door on Court 5, British hearts also soared when James Turner, with his frenzied first serve, raced through the first set 6–1 against Karel Novacek, a heftily built Czechoslovakian with no mean serve of his own, ranked more than 250 places above him. Novacek eventually tamed the Turner onslaught, however, to win in five sets.

As the sun almost reluctantly set, Chris Bailey just had time to make it two sets all against another Czechoslovakian, Josef Cihak, and there was much excitement on Court 1, as the clock ticked beyond 9 pm, when Andrew Castle staged a spirited rally to take the second set from 1985 runner-up Kevin Curren. Hope of further exciting British progress the following day, therefore, but not so for 14th seed Andrei Chesnokov, who has still to impress Wimbledon in the way he knows he can. The Russian was served out by Brad Drewett, an Australian far more attuned to the conditions, 6–4, 7–6, 6–0. It had been a long but highly rewarding start.

Jeremy Bates returns an autograph-hunter's pen after safely negotiating the first round.

Hard though he tried, Andrei Chesnokov, the 14th seed, could not resist Australian Brad Drewett's sharper grass-court play.

Sergi Bruguera (right) found his first Wimbledon visit quite a sweat. He was allowed only seven games by Amos Mansdorf.

D A Y

2

Tuesday 27 June

Ladies' Day, with all top five seeds making their first appearance, was overshadowed by a man who has been the centre of attraction many times for many different reasons over the years – John Patrick McEnroe. On a cool, sometimes damp day, as low pressure reached London SW19 earlier than the weather experts had indicated and there was no play until just after 2 pm, McEnroe suddenly produced a classically dramatic performance, which suggested that perhaps after all he would be right and everyone else, who had said he would never be able to return as champion, would be gloriously proved wrong.

McEnroe, without a Grand Slam title anywhere to his name since 1984, had drawn probably the toughest first-round challenge of any of the seeds – Darren Cahill, 23, an Australian with precisely the sort of game and equally solid temperament which could ruffle the three-times former champion. In the end, a packed spellbound Centre Court crowd erupted in noisy salute for the American, who had prepared harder and longer than ever before on grass for The Championships, bypassing Paris. With two rasping aces, McEnroe finally survived a memorable challenge from Cahill, 4–6, 4–6, 6–2, 6–3, 8–6.

It was the first time in an always colourful, invariably controversial career that McEnroe had won a match from two sets down. While perhaps not quite as amazing as the Jimmy Connors comeback from two sets and 1–4 down against Mikael Pernfors on the same stage two years earlier, it was still a comeback of epic proportions.

When McEnroe double-faulted twice in the opening game of the third set, just as he had done on the way to losing the opening game of the first two sets, he looked on course for his first opening round defeat since 1978. Cahill at the time was playing immaculately and McEnroe, who was prowling about the turf with increasing irritation, was clearly in the process of digging his own grave.

McEnroe's serve was the main problem. 'I just felt I wasn't into it at the start. I wasn't moving properly and I felt paralysed, mentally and physically,' he said. There had been 16 double faults, even more stoic looks and much pursing of the lips as he tried to suppress his inner torment. His escape in that first game of the third set when, despite his chances, Cahill was unable to get an initial service break as in the opening two sets, was the starting point of McEnroe's transformation. A flurry of superb returns made it 2–0 for him, when he could have been 0–2, and from then on, slowly at first, McEnroe began to revive those splendid memories from the past with brilliant lobs, touch volleys and backhand service returns taken so early that even many of Cahill's best efforts were rapidly driven straight back past him.

It lasted 3 hours 22 minutes. The 55-minute rain delay immediately after Cahill had broken for 2–1 in the opening set had been more of an irritant than a factor. Twice in the final set McEnroe had to serve to stay in the hunt, but apart from his skill and courage there was other support he could rely on. 'The crowd was with him. He's well liked over here in England . . . for some reason,' observed Cahill with a degree of disappointment, both about that and the outcome. It was not the last time McEnroe was to be at odds with an Australian during the fortnight. For the moment, though, he was happy to have come through with a performance which, like the day, brightened as it went on. As McEnroe said,

John McEnroe performed quite a balancing act before completing his greatest Wimbledon comeback, from two sets down against Darren Cahill.

Darren Cahill tried to chase down every point against John McEnroe but sometimes had to take a breather.

'Wimbledon is probably the toughest tournament in the world. That's what makes it so great. Every kind of pressure is there.'

Not that there was much pressure on the leading ladies. Between them, Steffi Graf, Martina Navratilova, Chris Evert, Gabriela Sabatini and Zina Garrison dropped only 14 games in ten sets. Miss Graf's 49-minute victory over Britain's Julie Salmon, ranked 212, was marginally faster than those recorded by former champions Mrs Evert and Miss Navratilova, but three minutes slower than that of Miss Sabatini. She rounded off the Centre Court programme by defeating Australian veteran, Dianne Balestrat, 6–1, 6–0. Miss Garrison's 6–1, 6–2 defeat of Japan's Kimiko Date took almost three hours, but only because this was one of a host of matches interrupted by rain.

Seeking a record ninth title, Miss Navratilova, who on the eve of The Championships had made her now-customary personal visit to Centre Court to pluck a few blades of grass (from outside the playing area, of course) to keep in her tennis bag for luck, was, like McEnroe, better prepared than in any previous year. She had won 11 matches on grass over the previous two weeks.

Her confidence, she proclaimed, after beating 6–3, 6–2 Canada's Jill Hetherington, who had startled her occasionally with flourishing returns, could not have been higher.

On one of those days when so many players had so much they clearly wanted to discuss, even though little of it related to the matches they had just played, Miss Navratilova reminded us once again of her everlasting romance with Wimbledon. When asked the inevitable question about keeping grass courts, she made an impassioned plea in support of them. 'Why change it? There will be nothing to gain by changing. If every court in the world was the same it might be convenient but it would be dreadfully boring.'

Then, just to embrace still tighter the tournament which she regards as unique (so much so that she has four of the old seats which were replaced on Centre Court a few years ago on the patio of her home in Aspen, Colorado), Miss Navratilova said, 'I'm still as excited about playing here as the very first time. That is the beauty of it. You never get tired of it. It's like what I've read about the golfers playing the Masters. Driving up Magnolia Drive they get the same

'Fancy having sun in your eyes at Wimbledon' Chris Evert could be forgiven for thinking.

*The net offered little protection for Julie Salmon
against Steffi Graf.*

Zina Garrison poised to strike against Japan's Kimiko Date.

Swedish qualifier, Henrik Holm, 20, whose father, Christer, was a Swedish Davis Cup player, had an impressive first-round win on his Wimbledon debut over South African Neil Broad.

feeling about playing golf there as tennis players do when they play tennis here.'

Day Two was not the exclusive prerogative of the famous. Others made their mark, mainly without fuss but often in splendid matches on outside courts, emphasizing once again how, for the first nine days at least, a ground admission ticket to Wimbledon must be one of the best value tickets in sport. Two men's matches in particular which fell into this category on this day were Robert Seguso's victory, 9–7 in the fifth, over fellow American Jim Courier, and the triple tie-break defeat of another outstandingly promising young American, David Wheaton, by Sweden's Jonas Svensson. There had, however, been service breaks along the way.

There was some unfinished and much new business to be done by British players, with mixed results. The day began disappointingly when Jo Durie, the British number two, was forced to withdraw following a recurrence of a back injury. Her place in the draw went to 'lucky loser' Giselle Miro from Brazil, who took her chance with relish to beat South Africa's Elna Reinach, 6–1, 6–3, although that was as far as she got.

In the second round she had to play Anne Hobbs, currently 577 in the world rankings. After a wretched spell of injury, which meant she was unable to play at all during 1988 when she was the British number one, Miss Hobbs marked her return with a tense 6–7, 6–4, 6–4 win against Australian Michelle Jaggard. 'This means the world to me. It's a second lease of life,' said Miss Hobbs, who was quickly joined in the second round by Sara Gomer and Clare Wood. Miss Gomer, successor to Miss Hobbs as British number one, easily beat the American, Leigh-Anne Eldredge, 6–3, 6–2, while Miss Wood had a surprisingly easy 6–0, 6–2 victory over Australian qualifier Tracey Morton.

Yet the main British rejoicing focused upon 6ft 5in Chris Bailey who, having trailed 1–3 in the fourth set before levelling his match with Czechoslovakia's Josef Cihak the night before, went on to complete a powerful serve and volley victory, 7–5, 6–7, 3–6, 6–3, 6–4. The crucial

No, it's not an old photograph of Martina Navratilova…but one of the next generation of Czechoslovakian players, Radka Zrubakova, as she lost to Hana Mandlikova.

moment came at 3–3 in the final set when Bailey broke, helped by two quality passing shots and then an exuberant running forehand down the line, accompanied by a yell of 'C'mon' to himself, as he did so.

Cihak saved the first of two match points with a superb lob and the next with a fierce backhand return, but Bailey gritted his teeth and produced two more magnificent winning serves to deserve the cheers which rang round Court 2.

Nick Brown's hopes of sustaining his good run at Bristol, where he had reached the final, ended in straight sets against qualifier Greg Holmes, although when the relative experience of the two players was considered it was hardly surprising; nor was Andrew Castle's ultimate 6–2, 4–6, 7–6, 6–3 loss to Kevin Curren.

Yet Castle had chances. Although he trailed 3–5 soon after they resumed at one set all overnight, he broke back to lead 6–5, only to

Britain's Anne Hobbs quickly settled back into her stride after a year out with injury.

Chris Bailey (right) determinedly completed a first-round victory over Czechoslovakia's Josef Cihak.

squander three set points. The second was a cruel blow. The ball hit the tape and fell back agonizingly on his side of the net. 'This is a game about inches,' the Taunton player commented philosophically.

Perhaps the happiest winner on Day Two was Wendy Turnbull. Officially she had retired from singles in January, when there were presentations on court to her at the Australian Open. For some, however, the lure of playing at Wimbledon just one more time remains irresistible. Like Chris Evert and Jimmy Connors, Wendy first played there in 1972. Wimbledon acknowledged her contribution with the provision of a wild card, and although having slipped to 282 in the rankings, 'rabbit' – as she has always affectionately been known on the circuit – scampered round the court quickly enough to beat the French player, Pascale Paradis, 13 years her junior, 6–4, 6–1.

Clare Wood (overleaf left) looked assured against Australian Tracey Morton, while even at 36, Wendy

Turnbull's enthusiasm was undiminished.

D A Y

3

Wednesday 28 June

The grey clouds shrouding Day Three at Wimbledon not only seemed appropriate in view of the rail strike, which accounted for the crowd figure of 33,525 being 3,415 down on the same day the previous year, but served as a poignant epitaph for Jimmy Connors, the swashbuckling hero of so many great performances, as he bowed out in the second round.

Pages of tennis history are regularly turned at Wimbledon. Connors was within shouting distance of completing another when, in his 50th Grand Slam tournament since he first appeared at the US Open in 1970, the champion of 1974 and 1982 was beaten by fellow American Dan Goldie. In his 98th match at an event where his 82 singles victories surpass those achieved by any other man, the old warrior, at 36, had to give second best, physically, to Goldie, from Sioux City, who until this year had not won a match at The Championships in three visits.

The packed crowd on Court 1, which had earlier been enchanted by their first significant sight of Arantxa Sanchez Vicario, the new teenage heroine of Spain and the French Open champion, willed Connors to succeed. They cheered almost every point he won, especially in the fourth set, but although the Connors spirit was there, he no longer had the stamina to produce more than fleeting glimpses of the old magic. He was beaten 7–6, 5–7, 6–4, 6–2. Goldie, the world's number 48 at the time, is, like Connors (though 14 years later), a former winner of the NCAA title in the United States and his power-based game is well crafted to succeed on grass.

Connors was twice a break up in the first set, but lost it, while in the third set he was four times unable to take break points. Goldie took his first break point in the tenth game after Connors double-faulted at 40–30 and then made two of those forehand errors which increasingly, in recent years, have been his downfall. Not even the winner of 107 titles round the world in 18 years can beat the passage of time.

Will he be back? As ever, Connors would not say. 'I'll play the rest of the year and then see what happens,' he remarked, knowing only too well that by 1990 he might be hard-pressed to be seeded.

If Ivan Lendl was looking for an easy passage and encouragement after the way he had been forced to toil in the first round, neither was forthcoming against the little-known Swedish player, Ronnie Bathman, 30, who actually took the first set. You had to run your finger down the world rankings to the 311th name on the list to find Bathman who, but for reaching the semi-finals of the doubles in Paris, might have changed his mind about qualifying and moved full time into the insurance company for which he was already working between tournaments.

Although Lendl eventually stamped his authority forcibly on the match, in a fourth set lasting 24 minutes, to win 6–7, 6–3, 6–2, 6–2, until midway through the third set he looked distinctly uncomfortable. Only his serve, despite three double faults in the second game, offered any consistent comfort. He hit 21 aces, but nine double faults muted even his satisfaction with that.

Brad Gilbert joined the list of seeded players beaten in the first round. The American and Australia's John Fitzgerald had been locked at two sets all overnight, but from 2–2 in the fifth the man from 'down under' took complete charge to win 6–2, 7–5, 1–6, 3–6, 6–2. There was little doubt who had benefited most from the interruption.

Once again the late start to the day's play, caused by the rain, meant a late finish, while Boris Becker's match with Richard Matuszewski never made it to court at all. Two other seeds, Miloslav Mecir and Aaron Krickstein, would probably

have wished for a similar respite. Mecir just managed to grab the third set to keep his hopes alive after losing the first two to Australian Mark Kratzmann, while Krickstein saved two match points in the fourth-set tie-break before resting for the night against Argentina's Javier Frana.

On the domestic front, the honours were divided between Valda Lake and Nick Fulwood. In the first men's singles match between two British players since Buster Mottram beat Robin Drysdale in 1981, the Derbyshire player beat former junior champion, Mark Petchey, 7–5, 6–1, 6–2. While a few courts away Chris Bailey was being blown off course by the raw serving power of Yugoslavia's Slobodan Zivojinovic, despite holding three points to take the third set and then saving three match points in a 13–11 third-set tie-break, Fulwood regularly imposed his stronger, more effective serve against Petchey.

Conditions everywhere were difficult. The light was never good, the wind often trouble-some and the courts still damp enough to make the ball keep low or skid by in alarming fashion. Fulwood wisely concentrated on tough serves, rather than the constant sorties to the net favoured by Petchey which left him so vulnerable to passing shots. The breakthrough came for Fulwood in the 12th game of the opening set, although Petchey, having just been beaten by a superb passing shot, was unfortunate at set point. A loose ball on the side of the court meant a delay between his first and second serves. He double-faulted.

Jeremy Bates had played confidently to take the opening set from Leif Shiras 6–4 but had allowed his concentration to wander into all sorts of wasteful directions as the American took the second set, before they joined the list of unfinished matches.

Valda Lake, playing determinedly against an opponent ranked 263 places above her, needed only four games to complete her 7–6, 3–6, 6–1 defeat of Yugoslavia's Sabrina Goles, which had started almost 24 hours earlier. The Devon girl benefited from deciding to play much more positively in the third set, taking the initiative as quickly as possible on each point instead of allowing her opponent to dictate the pattern and pace.

Mary Joe Fernandez had a difficult time progressing 6–4, 7–5 against Mary Lou Daniels, while Helen Kelesi from Canada became the first

Dan Goldie's power eventually wore down Jimmy Connors's always admirable resistance.

Mark Kratzmann kept plucking a host of early winners from his strings as he established a two-sets lead over Miloslav Mecir.

Britain's Valda Lake justified her wild card.

Mary Joe Fernandez had to work hard to beat Mary Lou Daniels, who well remembers what it was like to be a leading teenage player.

seed to fall in the women's singles when she went down 7–6, 7–5 to the American, Shaun Stafford. 'I don't feel comfortable on grass,' said the Canadian, stating the obvious. 'There's so much pressure on you when you have to try and do things which you are not sure you can do. It's the first time I've lost in the first round all year. It would have to be here!'

The star of Day Three, however, outshining even Monica Seles and Steffi Graf, already playing one round ahead of her, was clearly Miss Sanchez Vicario. Although the match was almost entirely devoid of volleys, the Spaniard's un-bridled joy as she moved steadfastly towards her first victory at Wimbledon in three attempts was infectious.

She beat another teenager, Jana Pospisilova from Czechoslovakia, 6–2, 7–5, in a match which provided almost as much difficulty in

pronouncing the names for umpire George Grime as it did in reality for Miss Sanchez Vicario, who had decided a few weeks earlier to add her mother's maiden name to her own, just as it has always been in Spain.

Miss Sanchez Vicario had cleared the first hurdle towards what everyone was assuming would be a re-match – though this time in the quarter-finals – against Miss Graf, whom she had beaten for the French title. Before that, however, there was an equally intriguing clash between Miss Graf and Miss Seles in prospect in the fourth round.

After her narrow escape against Brenda Schultz, Miss Seles had quickly asserted herself against Claudia Porwik, beating the West German 6–2, 6–4 in a match switched at the last minute to the Centre Court, although with so many other matches excitingly in the balance

elsewhere that evening, her success was shared by a sparse crowd.

Miss Graf had preceded her young challenger on to Centre Court and, as usual, did not occupy the court for long. She took just 43 minutes to beat the American teenager, Kimberly Kessaris, 16, winner of the Australian junior title in January, 6–2, 6–1.

Kevin Curren demonstrated that his serve could still be a match-winner as he beat Andrew Castle.

Gabriela Sabatini dropped only one game against
Dianne Balestrat.

D A Y

4

Thursday 29 June

Gabriela Sabatini had been in two minds about competing at Wimbledon this time. The inner doubts she felt, not only about a mental tiredness from travelling and living mainly out of suitcases when you are still a teenager, coupled with her lack of confidence about playing on grass, proved to have been justified when she was beaten, unsurprisingly, by Ros Fairbank on Day Four.

Although the third-seeded Argentinian had won four of her five previous matches against the recently married, California-based South African, this was the first time they had met on grass – and that was the crucial difference. While Miss Sabatini had returned to Florida after Paris and was therefore inevitably short of match practice, let alone on grass, Miss Fairbank had the week before been a semi-finalist at Eastbourne.

While she, for the most part, made the task look easy, moving in behind her serves to put away a plentiful supply of volleys, Miss Sabatini too often hesitated and then faltered from the back of the court. Only when on the point of victory did Miss Fairbank's control waver. Serving for the match she was 0–40, but then stamped her foot in personal annoyance and won the next five points to triumph 6–4, 6–3.

This was not the only seeding upset on a day once more cramped by the weather. It was 3.18 pm before a ball was hit anywhere but then, for close on six hours, there was action and

Gabriela Sabatini (right) masks her disappointment as she congratulates Ros Fairbank, after being unable to resist her opponent's serve and volley style.

excitement almost everywhere as three other seeds, Zina Garrison, Susan Sloane and Mikael Pernfors, were beaten and two others, Pam Shriver and Miloslav Mecir, went within a point of defeat.

Far more surprising than Miss Sabatini's exit, not least in ranking terms, was the 1–6, 6–2, 7–5 loss by fifth-seeded Miss Garrison to the Australian, Louise Field, ranked 121. Both players were unmistakably nervous and this was reflected by the topsy-turvy nature of the play and by the score. In the final set Miss Garrison pulled back from 0–5 to 5–5, saving four match points in the process, but just when it seemed as if she could go on to complete a famous recovery, the American found herself under pressure again, as Miss Field steadied herself and found the space and timing she needed to come up with more winning passes.

Several of the Australian cricketers, taking a day off from trouncing England, added to the antipodean cheers for Miss Field, but they were denied the even more notable triumph they were expecting on Court 2 when Mark Kratzmann, who often wears an Australian cricket cap, reached match point against seventh-seeded Miloslav Mecir. Kratzmann, junior champion in 1984, will recall the loss of this often classic contest as just as much a missed opportunity as that experienced by his doubles partner, Darren Cahill, against John McEnroe two days before.

In a match which had been halted with Kratzmann leading by two sets to one overnight, he led 5–3 in the fourth set and was just two points away from victory when his serve deserted him. Mecir, a 1988 semi-finalist, took 17 of the next 18 points, but in the tenth game of the final set he double-faulted to give the Australian match point. Mecir survived only because Kratzmann's next solid return hit the tape but

dropped back on his side of the net. He won only two more points. 'The Big Cat', as fellow players have dubbed their lean and languid Czechoslovakian colleague with the huge stride and reach, had used up another of his lives.

Miss Shriver, whose tennis earlier in 1989 had lacked much of its old instinctive sparkle, even when she was making mistakes, enjoyed what seemed rather more than a narrow escape against Britain's Sara Gomer out on Court 14. Miss Shriver, a semi-finalist in the two previous years, was serving at 3–5, 0–15 in the deciding set when, by all accounts, she hit a smash well beyond the baseline, although there was no call and no over-rule. Even so, Miss Gomer still had two match points later in the game, both of which she squandered by pushing backhands into the net, and a third in the next game which Miss Shriver saved in handsome style.

Miss Shriver went on to win 6–4, 3–6, 8–6, and with Clare Wood and Valda Lake losing respectively to the Americans, Patty Fendick and Gretchen Magers (who was to go on to enjoy her best Wimbledon), the only British joy in the

women's singles came from the feisty Anne Hobbs. She rallied from 0–4 in the third set to beat Brazil's Giselle Miro, 5–7, 6–2, 6–4, for the right to step back into the limelight again with a third-round match against Chris Evert.

On the other hand there was no joy for Jeremy Bates. Clearly still perturbed by the three points he had wasted to take an overnight two sets lead against Leif Shiras, he crumbled in only a further 65 minutes and was beaten 4–6, 7–5, 6–3, 6–2. 'I can't remember returning serve so badly. All in all I was pretty sick about the way I played,' said Bates. So too were many of his supporters who had seen it all happen so often before.

Elsewhere, Aaron Krickstein clambered safely into the third round after tugging the safety harness tightly enough when two match points down overnight against Javier Frana. Laura Gildemeister and Peter Lundgren emphasized the vulnerability of lower seeds by beating Miss Sloane and Pernfors respectively. And on Court 14 Arantxa Sanchez Vicario showed how quickly she was learning to use the full width and length of the court with an attractive combination

Mikael Pernfors never fully picked himself up after losing a first-set tie-break to fellow Swede Peter Lundgren.

Louise Field leaves to celebrate her fine win over fifth-seeded Zina Garrison.

of drop shots, lobs and fierce groundstrokes (though still hardly a volley), as she beat France's Julie Halard 6–4, 6–3.

These, with all respect, though, remained the supporting cast. The principals, for the most part, went about their business on the show courts with increasing control and efficiency, with one notable exception, which I will come to later.

On Centre Court, for instance, Boris Becker fans enjoyed another display of forceful serving power from the man the bookmakers were still insisting was the clear favourite to take the men's singles title. Becker, firmly in control, except when he was forced to save three second-set points, beat the American, Richard Matuszewski, 6–3, 7–5, 6–4, and seemed to have plenty in reserve to take charge of everything happening around him. That included the inevitable controversy that erupted after he changed into a shirt almost entirely covered by a combination of green and blue stripes, at 3–2 in the third set, which clearly contravened Wimbledon's 'predominantly white' rule.

Nothing was said at the time, but Becker knew he had been in the wrong and was left in little doubt that his excuse – that he had no other fresh shirt in his bag – would not be acceptable another time. There are many who support Wimbledon's 'predominantly white' policy just as passionately as the retention of grass courts. It is perhaps worth remembering that in olden days coloured clothing was permitted. It was the players themselves, realizing that white clothing usually made them feel cooler, who began the white tradition.

The Becker match, delayed for more than an hour by drizzle, was followed by Chris Evert against the American-domiciled Hu Na, one of the first Chinese players to make their mark. Shockwaves began to filter to all corners of The All England Club as Mrs Evert's first-set deficit reached 1–5 and she four times found herself within a point of losing the set. Once she rediscovered the range and timing on her returns, however, she took nine consecutive games to move to a 7–5, 6–3 victory.

Over on Court 1, John McEnroe became locked in a fascinating three-hour struggle to overcome Richey Reneberg, the American, who had done well there before, including taking a set from Ivan Lendl. This time he deserved the set he took from

Richey Reneberg deserved the set he took from John McEnroe.

Boris Becker (far left) steam-rollered his way into the third round against Richard Matuszewski – but that shirt raised a few eyebrows.

the fifth seed, and indeed he should have taken another, before losing 6–3, 3–6, 6–3, 7–5, for he led 5–2 in the fourth. 'I don't think I'm playing at my best yet but winning is obviously the main thing,' said McEnroe, who added that he felt this was the first time in his three visits to Wimbledon since being champion in 1984 that he had 'a true opportunity' to win again. He was far from alone in that belief, even though harsh reality should have tempered some of the McEnroe fever which was beginning to develop.

Late in an exhausting day, after fourth-seeded Mats Wilander had moved into the third round without fuss, bother or much attention with a straight sets defeat of Karel Novacek, defending champion Stefan Edberg lost a set to Australian junior, Todd Woodbridge, who was stunning him with glorious backhand returns, but only after the Swede, 0–3 down in the first set, had taken the opening two sets in the gathering gloom.

Out on Court 2, however, there was extraordinary drama as Martina Navratilova not only lost the first set but trailed 1–3 in the second, before bad light eventually stopped play at one set all in her second-round match with Australian qualifier, Kristine Radford.

Miss Radford, 19, a sturdy right-hander from Sydney, was wearing one of the two pairs of specialist grass-court shoes that Miss Navratilova had given her after she had beaten her in the Dow Classic at Edgbaston two weeks earlier. Until the fifth game of the second set, 17th ranked Miss Radford was inspired. A natural serve and volleyer, she went for everything, including huge second serves, as she took the first set 6–3 and broke for 2–1 in the second with a spectacular backhand service return.

The former champion seemed bewildered. The harder she tried, the worse things seemed to get, until at last a brilliant backhand stop volley, which enabled her to break back to 3–3, began to turn the match round. Miss Radford took only five more points in that set, which Miss Navratilova won 6–3, but the former champion was still left with much to mull over during the night.

Andres Gomez contemplated what to try next against Michiel Schapers...but never came up with the right answer.

The scoreboard shows why Martina Navratilova was relieved to take an overnight break against Australian qualifier, Kristine Radford, who left to a standing ovation from a packed late-night crowd on Court 2.

D A Y

5

Friday 30 June

Unfinished matches one day at Wimbledon are slotted in as second matches on their respective courts in the Order of Play for the following day, so Martina Navratilova and her entourage, both official and unofficial, had an extra period of suspense before the nightmare, which almost overwhelmed her the previous evening, could be laid to rest.

Miss Navratilova took the final set which remained to be played 6–3, but she was still nervous and still struggling to come to terms with what was clearly an unreal situation for her, until Kristine Radford gave her the chance for a comforting break to 4–3, with two double faults. Even so Miss Navratilova still had to ward off a break point against her, but Miss Radford froze just when she held a golden opportunity to pass.

'Short of having match points against me, I don't think that could have been any tougher,' said Miss Navratilova. And casting her mind back a few hours she added, 'Everything that could have gone wrong last night, went wrong. I was very lucky and just happy to have finished at one set all.'

In the meantime, while ninth-seeded Natalia Zvereva was losing on the adjoining Court 3 to Sweden's Catarina Lindqvist, 7–6, 4–6, 6–4, with Miss Lindqvist's elegant, as well as eloquent backhand finally coming into full bloom when she was 0–3 in the third set, a marvellous

Martina Navratilova uttered more than a sigh of relief after finally overcoming Kristine Radford (far right), who again made a lively start, watched intently by young admirers.

'women's singles tussle was unfolding on Centre Court.

Part of the joy of watching the boisterous baseline battle between Arantxa Sanchez Vicario and the doughty Italian, Raffaella Reggi, driving away at each other for two hours or more, was that the errors were sometimes as spectacular and as enthusiastic as the winners. The Spaniard certainly lived dangerously, saving two match points before raising her arms in a mixture of triumph and relief to celebrate a 4–6, 6–3, 7–5 victory.

Neither player has yet fathomed the niceties of grass-court play. Miss Reggi's volleys are unpredictable, to say the least, and there are times when her serve is no more than the opening gambit in what she clearly expects to be a lengthy argument. Yet both give 100 per cent at all times, and this was clearly the toughest task Miss Sanchez Vicario had faced since Paris. Miss Reggi, who had beaten Mrs Evert at the Olympic Games in Seoul, recovered from 2–4 to take the first set and was 4–3, with a break up, in the deciding set when this fascinating struggle was briefly interrupted by more rain.

On resumption, Miss Reggi reached 5–3 and at 5–4 she served for the match, reaching match point for the first time when Miss Sanchez Vicario netted a high forehand. It was a daunting moment even for the newest and one of the youngest Grand Slam champions. Yet suddenly, in the middle of a testing, tormenting rally, the enchanting Spaniard, from almost on the baseline, slipped in a drop shot of the most audacious quality, as if it was something she did every day of her life. 'If she tried that shot a hundred times maybe it would work for her once or twice,' observed Miss Reggi with a mixture of admiration and despair.

When Miss Reggi put a forehand into the tramlines on her second match point, Miss Sanchez Vicario took eight of the next nine points to become the first Spaniard since Lilli D'Alvarez in 1927 to reach the last 16 of the event.

Monica Seles made a comfortable journey into her fourth-round re-match with defending champion, Steffi Graf, taking little more than an hour – though that is long by Miss Graf's standards – to beat Eva Sviglerova, 18, from

Natalia Zvereva was unable to resist Catarina Lindqvist's cunning style.

Joy for Arantxa Sanchez Vicario after saving two match points against the always defiant Raffaella Reggi.

Disappointment for Raffaella Reggi, who fought so hard.

Monica Seles in a balletic pose against Eva Sviglerova.

Czechoslovakia, 6–4, 6–3. Despite the three-year age gap she was giving away, Miss Seles hit harder and was always first to take the initiative with a drop shot or a lob. It was difficult enough for her opponent, without the lucky net cord by which Miss Seles completed the match.

For her part, Miss Graf once more looked in awesome form on Court 1, where she again took just 43 minutes to brush aside the challenge of Australia's Anne Minter, 6–1, 6–3. Meanwhile others joined her in the last 16, including Ros Fairbank, Helena Sukova – who recovered from losing the first set to another who has never fully justified her potential on these courts, Claudia Kohde-Kilsch – and the American, Lori McNeil.

In the men's singles, as the top three seeds, Ivan Lendl, Stefan Edberg and Boris Becker, moved relentlessly on towards a developing

showdown in the second week, the excitement came late on a day in which the women had naturally provided all the glamour and created the most entertaining matches.

The large numbers who stayed were more than rewarded by the way Slobodan Zivojinovic, the 1986 semi-finalist, thundered down 14 aces and even more brilliant returns on Centre Court to beat Miloslav Mecir, the Olympic champion, 6–7, 6–1, 7–5, 6–3, despite a progressive elbow injury which was to force him to take a prolonged break from tennis when The Championships were over.

Both men had been restricted by back injuries earlier in the year, but one would hardly have realized that from the style of this fine contest, although Mecir, after breaking back in the tenth game of the first set and then taking the tie-break

Kevin Curren tries to shrug off the occasional
setback against Milan Srejber.

Slobodan Zivojinovic (overleaf left) thrilled the
Centre Court with his power, which was too much
for Miloslav Mecir.

7–2 when his opponent was foot-faulted on a second serve, never had the opportunity of break point again. In the fourth set, as the light faded, Zivojinovic mixed his power and touch with enormous confidence. No one could have played a better winning shot than the magnificent lob which had Mecir haring back to the baseline, only to return the ball into the net.

Mecir's frustration was understandable, but no doubt minor compared with that of Kevin Curren, the 12th seed who had three match points before going down 4–6, 6–3, 5–7, 7–6, 6–3 to Leif Shiras, then ranked a modest 140, or of Holland's Tom Nijssen. He had four match points before losing a 28-game fifth set, the longest in singles at Wimbledon '89, to David Pate from the United States 6–4, 2–6, 1–6, 7–6, 15–13.

Earlier, the developing authority of Lendl,

Edberg and Becker was emphasized. 'I believe I'm getting better every day,' said Lendl after following Miss Navratilova on to the supposedly notorious Court 2 and admitting that he had enjoyed the experience. Lendl, whose game really took off against 115th-ranked Tomas Carbonell from Spain, after rain delayed the middle of the second set, said, 'I like the court. The surface is better for my game . . . harder and quicker, so when I hit my volleys, they skid away from the guy.' Carbonell, competing at Wimbledon for the first time, often hit stunning service returns, although he was never a major threat and Lendl, who conceded only six points on serve in the third set, won 7–6, 6–3, 6–1.

Edberg, whose match with Todd Woodbridge, 18, a talented Australian qualifier, had been delayed overnight, was hardly as exuberant about his form after completing a 6–4, 6–4, 1–6,

7–6 win. But then he seldom is. The breakthrough for Edberg came at 5–5 in the fourth-set tie-break when he reached wide to hit a brilliant forehand service return down the line and then climaxed his success with a typically confident and authorative volley.

A second-set tie-break, which Becker won 7–1 by playing what he called his best seven points of the match, was the key to the former champion's 7–5, 7–6, 6–3 defeat on Court 1 of Jan Gunnarsson, who is no mean competitor in any company and, throughout the first two hard-

Boris Becker strode into the fourth round with more heavy serving against Jan Gunnarsson.

hitting sets, was never far away from putting the West German in real trouble.

Michael Chang could have been forgiven if thoughts of his astonishing French Open triumph were still racing through his shrewd mind as he beat Haiti's Ronald Agenor, 4–6, 6–2, 6–1, 7–5, for this was one of the men he had eliminated during his historic achievement at Roland Garros.

In fact Chang was determined to push all such memories into the background. 'If I dwell on what happened there I'll be side-tracked and not able to produce my best here,' said the youngster, who took time to cope with Agenor's huge, lashed forehand drives, especially while his own serve was wavering. Both were reluctant to expose their forecourt limitations. For most of the first two sets the rallies were more suited to clay than grass, but with Chang returning most of Agenor's best serves, the Chinese-American eventually felt it was time to start testing the water near the net. From 0–1 in the second set he won 15 of the next 17 games to reach 3–0 in the fourth.

Britain's interest in the men's singles, which had at least lasted one round longer than the previous year, ended when qualifier Nick Fulwood ran out of big serves against the chunky American, Paul Chamberlin. Yet despite failing to become the first British player to reach the fourth round since Buster Mottram in 1982, Fulwood had the satisfaction of knowing that he had broken into the world's top 200 for the first time – to reach 176, in fact.

After a splendid first set, when he astutely mixed serve and volley winners with crisp, accurate play from the back of the court, it all started to drift away from Fulwood once he lost the second point of the second-set tie-break. At that moment, Chamberlin hit a stinging service return which was clearly going to be a winner even before the ball clipped the top of the tape as it went over.

'Don't all clap at once,' said Chamberlin to a large but mainly restrained crowd on Court 13, which was naturally hoping for, but never quite believing in, a British success. Chamberlin, 27, an all-round sportsman who had just broken into the top 100 for the first time, though he would certainly be a contender for the top ten among the grunters, then increasingly took charge to win 3–6, 7–6, 6–4, 6–2.

After losing the first set, Michael Chang quickly sensed he could repeat his French Open victory over Ronald Agenor.

D A Y

6

Saturday 1 July

The longest recorded match in the history of The Championships, 5 hours 28 minutes, was completed on Day Six, yet it attracted surprisingly little attention, partly no doubt because it involved two lesser-ranked challengers, Greg Holmes and Todd Witsken, both from the United States, and partly because it was tucked away on Court 17.

It had started on Day Four and ended some 41 hours later with a thrilling victory for qualifier Holmes when he hammered a double-handed forehand past the incoming Witsken on his sixth match point to complete a 5–7, 6–4, 7–6, 4–6, 14–12 victory.

The first stoppage had come through bad light late on Day Four. On Day Five, when there were also four brief interruptions for drizzle, play was suspended for a sixth time when Holmes, who had slipped from 27 at his peak to 309 in the world rankings, squandered two match points just after 9 pm, when Witsken eventually held to make it 9–9.

The first six games after that yielded only six points against the serve and then Witsken defiantly saved three more match points before the net cord, which ultimately carried his opponent to match point number six, ended his resolve. They had played 71 games, considerably less than the record 112 by Pancho Gonzales and Charlie Pasarell in 1969, but that was in the days

before there were chairs for players to rest on at change-overs and that match lasted only 5 hours 12 minutes.

Holmes had rather less time than that – in fact just under two hours – to savour his contribution to the history of Wimbledon before he had to return to court for his third-round match with 16th-seeded Amos Mansdorf from Israel. Not surprisingly he was beaten comprehensively and swiftly, 6–2, 6–4, 6–2.

Meanwhile at the more exalted end of the tournament Martina Navratilova, striving for that record ninth title, and John McEnroe, excited simply by the prospect of winning again, kept company with Stefan Edberg, Mats Wilander and Michael Chang in feeling well satisfied with their first week's work.

Miss Navratilova and McEnroe in particular felt they had found their best form, as first one overwhelmed the teenage Australian, Nicole Provis, 6–0, 6–3, and then the other, roared on by the Centre Court crowd, swept commandingly past Californian Jim Pugh, 6–3, 6–4, 6–2.

With the exception of the fourth game of the second set, when he double-faulted twice and was broken, McEnroe's serving was magnificent and his volleying just as confident and secure.

The gates had been closed at 1.08 pm, and those able to see the former champion relished the sight of him in such splendid fettle against his 77th-ranked opponent, double-handed on both sides and best known for his doubles triumphs. Pugh had more chances than the score implies, but missed too many backhand volleys. Nor could he ever match McEnroe's scoring power on serve.

Miss Navratilova must have expected a sterner challenge from Miss Provis, but the second seed played as if the match which ended the day before, against Kristine Radford, had just been a bad dream. She dropped only 12 points in a first set lasting a mere 19 minutes and permitted only one of those games even to reach deuce. 'That was the best I have served for a long time,' she said. 'Today my attitude was much more positive. The fact that I was playing on Centre Court helped. It was the first time I've been there this year and I don't really feel I'm in the tournament until I get on Centre Court. When you think about Wimbledon, you automatically think about playing on Centre Court. Once I knew this match would be there, I was jumping

Nicole Provis found herself tied up in knots by Martina Navratilova.

A strong guard for John McEnroe as he left Court 14 after a doubles victory with Jakob Hlasek a few hours after police were alerted to a death threat against him, *on the day he also beat Jim Pugh in a Centre Court singles.*

Jim Pugh's boldness was not enough.

for joy.' Her contentment was obvious.

That win took Miss Navratilova into a fourth-round meeting with another former Czechoslovakian, Hana Mandlikova, now also playing under the Australian flag. Miss Mandlikova, runner-up in 1981 and 1986 but still just as likely to score own goals in matches she has dominated, reached the last 16 out on Court 2 with a 6–2, 6–4 defeat of the left-handed American, Donna Faber, who was another taking part in the tournament for the first time.

Just occasionally there were glorious glimpses of that impressive power and touch which ought to have brought Miss Mandlikova far more success than she has recorded. Yet there is a will-o'-the-wisp mood within her which continues to make her vulnerable, so that so much glittering talent just drains away.

The only seed to vanish on this middle Saturday was the number eight in the women's singles, Pam Shriver. She lost a two and a half hour marathon 6–2, 2–6, 12–10 to Gretchen Magers, ranked 40th in the world, a long-time disciple of former champion Evonne Goolagong and one of the few players who still favours an old-fashioned visor when playing.

For Miss Shriver it was the all too familiar pattern of early confidence becoming dissipated and then being replaced by self-doubt. Mrs Magers's backhand, in particular, perked up in the third set, though she wasted four match points before Miss Shriver obliged by dumping another forehand into the net.

It was the first time Mrs Magers had beaten an opponent ranked among the world's top ten. 'I can't really remember what happened towards the end. I was in a whirl,' she said. Miss Shriver was perfectly clear why it had all gone so wrong for her in recent months. 'I thought I could play social tennis and get away with it,' she remarked. 'But you've just got to compete at the highest level all year round these days. I've got to make a choice. I'm considering my future now as a singles player.'

Among other seeds, Mary Joe Fernandez and Jana Novotna also advanced and so too, naturally enough, did Chris Evert, who beat Anne Hobbs 6–4, 6–1 to remove the last British interest from either of the singles events. Miss Hobbs fought hard in the opening set when the three-times former champion was again struggling to find her timing and the British player actually led 3–2.

From then on, however, it all became rather a formality.

Edberg, through a succession of circumstances beyond anyone's direct control, found himself once more the last act of the day on an attractive Centre Court bill, beating Scott Davis 6–3, 6–4, 4–6, 6–2. The match finished at 8.53 pm with the light then appreciably better than it had been during the third set, when ominous black clouds passed over, leaving the chief source of illumination coming from the flashbulbs on spectators' cameras. 'This is precisely the kind of tough match I need at this stage of the tournament,' remarked Edberg, who was relieved that they had been able to finish, rather than having to wait until the Monday before they could resume.

Two special guests on Court 1 for most of Day Six had been two pupils from Myton School in Warwick, Matti Tucker and Kamaldeep Rhandawa. While queuing for admission to the ground the two girls had stumbled across a pair of Centre Court tickets lying in the road. Despite the immediate attention of nearby ticket touts, who discovered what had happened and offered them £150, they insisted on the tickets being handed to an All England Club steward. He, in turn, found seats for them on Court 1 where, among other rewards, they were able to watch the latest chapter in the remarkable Michael Chang story.

The boy who so many, including John McEnroe, had insisted, sometimes in extravagant terms, would struggle to play on grass, fought back from 0–4 and 1–5 in the third set to beat Michiel Schapers of Holland, 4–6, 6–3, 7–5, 7–5, with some of the most enthralling tennis of the first week.

For six games from 1–5 Chang lifted his play in a way matched only in recent times by Steffi Graf's turbo-powered take-off from a set and 0–2 down against Martina Navratilova in the 1988 final. 'I made sure I concentrated on every point and didn't make an error,' said Chang, whose returns, both crosscourt and down the line, were hit with breathtaking pace and clinical accuracy. In particular he kept them dipping low, just over the net, making them doubly difficult for Schapers, a tall man, to respond to.

Because of the weather, which interrupted play to some extent or another on four of the first five days, doubles matches enjoyed limited exposure in the first week, but when they did get

Hana Mandlikova's serve worked well against Donna Faber.

going there was immediately an upset in the first round of the men's doubles when Britain's James Turner and Stephen Botfield, always capable of such a performance, beat sixth-seeded Paul Annacone and Christo Van Rensburg, 7–5, 6–3, 7–5.

No doubt Van Rensburg's thoughts were still on his three-hour singles triumph in a fluctuating match against Brad Drewett earlier in the day. The deciding set had been a real thriller. Van

Old-timers admired the style of Gretchen Magers as she drove her way to victory over Pam Shriver (left).

Rensburg produced two brilliant passing shots to earn himself three match points at 9–8. Drewett saved the first with a crisp forehand volley but was too long with a similar shot on the next point, and the South African was a 6–3, 2–6, 2–6, 6–2, 10–8 winner.

Next in line for him would be Mats Wilander who, despite being, along with Becker, the only player to reach the second week in the men's singles without dropping a set, had barely

Anne Hobbs produced a plucky first set against Chris Evert.

Tough going for Scott Davis against Stefan Edberg.

warranted a mention by that stage, except from Swedish journalists.

Wilander looked efficiently impressive as he beat the young Australian, Jason Stoltenberg, 6–3, 6–3, 6–3, and was dismissive of the 25–1 betting odds being offered against him. 'If I didn't rate my chances higher than that I'd be on the next plane home,' he said, while admitting that he had still to face his first challenge from a genuine grass-court player.

The scene was being set nicely for the second week. If only the weather would also play the game!

Anguish for Michiel Schapers as he was beaten by yet another Michael Chang winner.

Jason Stoltenberg became the third straight sets victim of Mats Wilander.

D A Y

7

Monday 3 July

It was the first time since 1983 that Day Seven reduced the women's singles to a field of eight containing only four seeds. Ros Fairbank, Laura Golarsa, Catarina Lindqvist and Gretchen Magers were the outsiders, gate-crashing the party, while in the men's singles Paul Chamberlin and Dan Goldie were the only survivors who could fall into that category.

Yet their efforts were overshadowed partly by the manner in which Michael Chang was given a few lessons in the hitherto masked grass-court facts of life, but more especially because John McEnroe prompted some memories of the past, for too many of the wrong reasons, as he reached the quarter-finals for the first time since 1985.

McEnroe beat John Fitzgerald, one of those thoroughly genuine, down-to-earth Australians who calls almost everyone 'mate', 6–3, 0–6, 6–4, 6–4, in a 2 hour 11 minute contest which ended with him calling the American anything but 'mate'. Fitzgerald was incensed by what he regarded as McEnroe's deliberate attempts to distract him, especially when he had pulled back from 0–4 to 3–4 in the first set. With Fitzgerald poised at 40–15 to make it 4–4, McEnroe showed what could only be called a prolonged reluctance to receive serve.

'I thought the receiver, as well as the server, had 30 seconds to prepare himself,' explained McEnroe later, but many in the crowd –

remembering how well versed he has been about the rules in the past – booed. 'Every time I go to serve, he stops me. It's up to you to keep the game going,' Fitzgerald told West German umpire, Rudi Berger. Sensing injustice, Berger issued a code violation, but that only encouraged McEnroe to walk slowly to the net and engage the official in a lengthy explanation of his action, while the Australian stewed on the baseline before once more losing the next point.

The noise which McEnroe said he could hear emanating from the refrigeration system, keeping the new balls cool at the side of the court, gave the American another chance for a delay, although perhaps anyone who has been the subject of a death threat might be forgiven for expressing alarm at the slightest ticking noise. Be that as it may, Fitzgerald went about as far as he dared later in his criticism of McEnroe's conduct. 'He gets away with it all the time,' he said. 'He tries to get people to believe that he's changed but that's ridiculous. He stretches the rules to the limit. It's hard to respect a guy like that.'

McEnroe later shrugged off the criticism as 'sour grapes' but could not have been left in any doubt that he had sacrificed a number of the friends he had been winning back, both with his approach and with his tennis, earlier in The Championships.

Curiously enough, it was the American rather than the Australian who took longest to regain his concentration after the first-set turmoil. With double faults costing him the second and fourth games, McEnroe lost the second set 0–6, the first time that had happened in any of his previous 57 matches at Wimbledon and only the fourth time in 166 matches at any of the Grand Slam tournaments.

It was only after Fitzgerald had also double-faulted to loose a wayward fifth game of the third set that the match turned back in McEnroe's favour and he once more began to demonstrate those swift returns and deft angles in which, in the right mood, he still specializes.

As for Chang, all the excitement which had been building up round Court 14, with enormous queues developing almost as soon as the gates opened, quickly evaporated when Tim Mayotte, the eighth seed and a semi-finalist in 1982, established an instant mastery which he never looked like yielding.

This was far more than simply 'a good big 'un

John McEnroe's inquisitive mood did not impress
John Fitzgerald, who was always keen to get on with
the business at hand.

Chief Supervisor, Ken Farrar, and Referee, Alan
Mills, keep a watching brief from the side of Court 1.

trouncing a good little 'un', although Mayotte's superiority in height, reach and strength was naturally an important factor. Here was the case of a teenager, who is still an apprentice in terms of grass-court play, unable to cope with the experience and knowledge of someone who has made a speciality of such matters.

It was not only Mayotte's archly angled serves, giving him so much scope for volleys, but also his bolder, more powerful returns which kept Chang under such intense pressure. Mayotte broke Chang's service three times in the first set, raced through the second in 28 minutes and went on to win 6–3, 6–1, 6–3. But few have any doubt that Chang, a fast learner, will be back, older and

Michael Chang kept fighting but his mother, Betty, knew it was the end of the road for him this year, when he met the resolute Tim Mayotte.

A chance that got away from Christo Van Rensburg when he was well placed to take a two sets lead against Mats Wilander, who had his own glamorous Swedish fans.

wiser, in years to come.

Mats Wilander continued his quiet but no less effective progress. The Swede, clearly more motivated than ever before to try and win the only Grand Slam title still eluding him, recovered from losing his first set in The Championships to beat Christo Van Rensburg, 3–6, 7–5, 7–5, 6–3. The match lasted 3 hours 4 minutes and suddenly turned after Wilander had saved a break point at 5–5 in the second set with a bold forehand volley. In the next game, Van Rensburg, who had led 40–15, threw away the chance of forcing a tie-break when he studiously allowed a service return to pass him only to discover, to his horror, that it dropped in. A fluffed forehand volley by the part-time magician, whose tricks were suddenly going horribly wrong, followed by another volley which left Wilander with an

inviting chance for a forehand pass, resulted in the fourth seed taking a set he had been on the point of conceding. He was never under threat again.

Top seed Ivan Lendl struggled for a while to come to terms with the heavily spun serves and brilliant double-handed returns of Peter Lundgren, the Swede who visually could easily be mistaken for Bjorn Borg, his idol. Lundgren, 24, twice broke a mentally frail Lendl in the first set and had a point for the second at 6–5, after recovering from 2–5, but the world number one bravely and wisely went in behind a return to force a critical error and followed that with aces in plenty as he went on to win 1–6, 7–6, 6–2, 6–4.

Stefan Edberg, that master of modesty about his own performances, spoke of 'a few good returns here and there' as he lifted his game

Appearances can be deceiving – and so can waistlines – as Peter Lundgren (left) demonstrates.

Leif Shiras (below), enjoyed his best Wimbledon yet until running into fellow American Paul Chamberlin.

*Dan Goldie proved durable enough to overcome
Slobodan Zivojinovic (above right).*

superbly from 1–3 in the opening set to beat Amos Mansdorf, 6–4, 6–3, 6–2, on a day which attracted 38,910 spectators, a record for any second Monday.

Boris Becker again came up with big shots on the biggest points with remarkable and telling consistency to beat Aaron Krickstein, 6–4, 6–4, 7–5, while to complete the last eight line-up, Paul Chamberlin beat Leif Shiras in the battle of unseeded Americans, 7–5, 6–4, 7–6, and Dan Goldie no doubt earned at least a whispered vote of thanks from Lendl by removing the giant-hitting Slobodan Zivojinovic, 6–4, 6–4, 7–6. Goldie surprised spectators around Court 13 by electing to receive the Yugoslav's normally intimidating serve in the first game. He proceeded to justify the decision by breaking serve in the opening game of each set. Not many people have ever done that against 'Bobo'.

Watching Steffi Graf overwhelm Monica Seles 6–0, 6–1 with one crushing forehand after another, one was left with the thought that the world champion was still irked by the memory of losing a set to the Florida-based Yugoslavian in Paris. 'I was really psyched up for this match,'

said Miss Graf, who allowed the girl with the giggle and the grunt only ten points in a first set which flashed by in 18 minutes. 'It's the second week of Wimbledon and now is the time it counts,' added Miss Graf with customary ruthlessness. Miss Seles ran her heart out but could not cope with her opponent's greater weight of shot.

There were flurries of brilliance from Hana Mandlikova but never enough for her to offer more than a token challenge to Miss Navratilova, especially after she delivered a double fault to go 2–1 down in the second set. With Gretchen Magers, who had knocked out Pam Shriver, beating Jo-Anne Faull, 6–7, 6–1, 6–0, the pert, snub-nosed Catarina Lindqvist having too many variations in her game for sixth-seeded Helena Sukova, and Ros Fairbank's greater grass-court

The fun also came to a halt, temporarily, for Monica Seles (overleaf left), when she lost to Steffi Graf, and for Hana Mandlikova, who was mainly kept on the defensive by Martina Navratilova.

experience too much for Mary Joe Fernandez, that meant there were no other seeds left in the former champion's half of the draw.

In what almost everyone was assuming to be Miss Graf's half of the draw, Arantxa Sanchez Vicario, the happy-go-lucky Spaniard, winning more admirers with every appearance, qualified to meet her in the quarter-finals with a 6–3, 2–6, 6–1 defeat of Lori McNeil, who, though lower-seeded, had been expected to do rather better.

In the first set she seemed surprised by the punishing returns and teasing use of the lob from the Spaniard, whose sunny attitude shines so richly through her tennis.

Chris Evert had a surprisingly easy 6–2, 6–2 victory over fellow American Patty Fendick, who once again failed to do justice either to herself or her potentially successful game on the big occasion. Meanwhile Laura Golarsa clearly benefited from massive vocal support from fellow countrymen around Court 4 as she became the first Italian since 1933 to reach the last eight here. A player with a deft touch, which enabled her to take frequent advantage of Jana Novotna's firmer hitting, Miss Golarsa, 21, won the first set from 1–4, saving three set points in the process.

Mrs Evert once again found herself facing an opponent she knew little about. 'But anyone who beats Novotna on grass must be pretty good,' she said sensibly.

By common consent, this was also a year in which the grass courts were not just 'pretty good' but superb, a tribute to the work of all the groundstaff, and in particular head groundsman Jim Thorn, who was awarded the British Empire Medal in this year's Queen's Birthday Honours.

After driving her way to victory over Lori McNeil, Arantxa Sanchez Vicario saluted her growing army of supporters and was more than happy to oblige with this request to autograph a shirt.

D A Y

8

Tuesday 4 July

On Day Eight Steffi Graf and Martina Navratilova moved one stage closer to the third consecutive Wimbledon final between them which almost everyone was expecting, but this was a day, perhaps even the last Wimbledon day, which truly belonged to Chris Evert.

With a sense of occasion which was so fitting, she went to within two points of defeat against Laura Golarsa, an Italian still taking her first tentative steps to stardom who had never before gone beyond the third round of any Grand Slam tournament, before something just clicked.

Almost at the very moment that Mrs Evert was questioning in her own mind whether she had any tennis left to give, she looked round a stunned, almost despairing crowd on Court 1 and told herself, 'This isn't the way I want to go out.'

Four games and 21 emotionally charged points later, the thousands of spectators who had been willing the former champion to produce one more flourish were on their feet, saluting a fairy-tale victory. Mrs Evert's father, Jimmy, the man who through most of her international career preferred to stay at home coaching in Florida, waiting for her to telephone him with reports on her progress, was among them. On this, only his third Wimbledon, he was probably prouder than them all.

Mrs Evert's courageous 6–3, 2–6, 7–5 victory not only made her a semi-finalist for the 17th time

in her 18th, and almost certainly farewell, appearance at The Championships, but also created Wimbledon history. For this triumph, carved unmistakably from the heart, was her 96th in 110 matches in the tournament, surpassing the record held by Billie-Jean King. A major proportion of them had been played on Centre Court. Somehow it would have seemed totally inappropriate, particularly at that moment, for her to have bowed out anywhere else.

Few, and not even Mrs Evert until she was prompted later, remembered that two years earlier Miss Golarsa, who went for her shots with a refreshing freedom, had held two points to take a first-set lead against one of the game's most enduring champions. That was in the second round and with Mrs Evert not conceding another game, the match was readily consigned to the list of routine results. This time it was all so different. With Miss Golarsa serving at 5–3, 30–0 in the final set, there was a chilling look of resignation on her opponent's drawn face.

Yet suddenly, almost miraculously, the back-hand, that source of so much strength and inspiration throughout Chris Evert's career, clicked back into spectacular shape, just when the curtain seemed to be falling. Three successive backhand winners, each greeted with a louder roar than the one before – and the last of them a magnificent piece of defiance, struck on the run, down the line – transformed a requiem into a celebration.

Recalling the last of that trio of memorable winners, Mrs Evert said later, 'That was the moment I felt inspired; the shot which put me back in contention. For the last four games I played the best that I have in the whole tournament. Until then my attitude had been more a case of "I can't believe this is happening to me." I thought to myself, this isn't the way I'd like to go out of the tournament if this is to be my last, which it probably will be. I felt really disappointed.' Only once before, when she trailed 7–6, 5–0, 40–15 against Nancy Richey in Indianapolis in 1975, had Mrs Evert, now 34, recovered from greater peril – though never in such significant or sentimental circumstances.

Not only the wind ruffled Chris Evert, before she recovered from 2–5 in the final set against Italy's Laura Golarsa (overleaf).

Early on, when she led by a set and a break, Mrs Evert and the crowd had little notion of the trauma to follow. When Miss Golarsa, surprisingly eager – for an Italian – to volley, decided to shorten the points and quicken the pace, taking eight successive games to lead 3–0 in the third, however, it looked like becoming the saddest possible ending to an era.

Miss Golarsa even had a point for 4–0, thanks to a double fault by the fast-tiring Mrs Evert, who at that stage was so often missing or failing to put away shots, including backhands, which a few years earlier would have been a formality. 'At 2–5 [and at deuce she was again only two points away from losing] I certainly didn't think I was going to win,' said Mrs Evert. 'I was asking myself, "Do I still have something in reserve? Is there still anything there?" Thank heavens there was.'

In almost any other circumstances, the way Miss Graf had to rely on every formidable forehand she could muster to ward off a spirited attack by Arantxa Sanchez Vicario would have attracted the star billing. Miss Graf won 7–5, 6–1 in 71 minutes, but only after a first set of 43 minutes which itself was as long as two of her completed earlier matches.

As at Roland Garros, the engaging Spaniard refused to be overawed by Miss Graf's renowned forehands. Once she had recovered from an early service break, she began returning them with almost equal power and certain equal length. Indeed, with Miss Sanchez Vicario clearly relishing her challenge and both players regularly hitting shots close enough to the lines to bring up chalk, it was a wonderfully fascinating tussle.

When Miss Sanchez Vicario broke in the ninth game so that she would then be serving for the opening set, there were some who began to wonder if perhaps we would see a repeat of what, at Roland Garros, had been one of the greatest upsets in the history of modern tennis.

Yet just when a fine match was poised to become a great one, the whirlwind efforts which Miss Sanchez Vicario had been making blew themselves out. She double-faulted to be broken to love, and took only two of the next 22 points during the course of losing seven successive games.

Miss Sanchez Vicario seemed troubled by a dubious-looking call which accentuated her problems in that tenth game, which was the

The spring was clearly back in Steffi Graf's step as she avenged her French Open defeat by Arantxa Sanchez Vicario.

Picnickers enjoy relaxing in Aaorangi Park.

Gretchen Magers's serve was never as effective as Martina Navratilova's.

poorest she played. But the reality was that Miss Graf tightened her game, particularly her serving, stepped up the pressure, and that explosive forehand found its target with renewed consistency and effectiveness.

As for Miss Navratilova, beating Gretchen Magers 6–1, 6–2, that was almost a sinecure by comparison. Mrs Magers clearly wanted to impress in this, the most significant match of her career, but from the moment she overhit twice in the opening game and was broken to 30 in the second, showing that she was even more nervous than her opponent, she must have begun to sense that it would not be her day.

Although Miss Navratilova, moving into the semi-finals for a 13th time, won comfortably, it was not an impressive or convincing perform-ance. She double-faulted twice in succession at 3–1 and was fortunate that Mrs Magers, a former leading junior, was unable to take advantage of any of the four chances she had in that game to unsettle the former champion still further.

You could feel Mrs Magers's sense of frustration when, on the first of those break points, she leaned back to wallop what should have been a winning forehand, only to dump it into the net. Watched attentively from the players' seats by Monica Seles, looking like a 'flapper' from the 1920s with her cloche hat and dangling earrings, Miss Navratilova strode smartly and with much relief to her chair when that seven-minute game ended, knowing better than anyone else how lucky she had been to escape. Had she lost that game, who knows? The ghost of Kristine Radford might have returned to haunt her.

In the match between two unseeded quarter-finalists, Catarina Lindqvist, ranked 25 in the world, beat Ros Fairbank, ranked 37, in straight sets, 7–5, 7–5, although it was far from being a straightforward match before she became the first Swedish player to reach a women's singles semi-final at Wimbledon.

Ros Fairbank and Catarina Lindqvist (right) both had moments of stress in their quarter-final.

Ros Fairbank and Catarina Lindqvist (right) both had moments of stress in their quarter-final.

Miss Lindqvist, coached by former British Davis Cup player, John Lloyd – who was confined to bed with the stomach upset which had forced him to concede a second-round match in the men's doubles with another of his pupils, Stephen Shaw – served for both sets at 5–4 but confessed to feeling 'a little nervous' on both occasions.

Although Miss Fairbank broke back to 5–5 both times, she then made costly mistakes in the game that followed, just as she had when 3–0 ahead, with two points for 4–0 in the first set. It was that sort of match.

Meanwhile, in the doubles, Rick Leach and Jim Pugh overcame the team many feel are next in line among top American partnerships, Jim Courier and Pete Sampras. Both members of the McEnroe clan also advanced, John with Jakob Hlasek, Patrick with Jim Grabb. John McEnroe and Hlasek had to finish a match with Americans Mike Depalmer and Gary Donnelly, which had been halted at two sets all overnight. It lasted another 18 games before the favourites eventually won 6–7, 6–4, 3–6, 7–5, 10–8, after a match which delighted the capacity crowd round Court 14. However, John had already warned that if the demands of the singles were putting undue strain on him, he might have to review his doubles commitment. The next round, he did just that.

9

Wednesday 5 July

There was more than a touch of irony about the fact that of the four quarter-finals in the men's singles, the one involving John McEnroe was the longest and the quietest, while another involving Stefan Edberg and Tim Mayotte, invariably two of the calmest, most level-headed players on the circuit, erupted into stormy controversy.

Not that a bewildered Edberg played more than a watching brief at the moment when Mayotte, much to his chagrin later, lost his self-control and that 'Gentleman Tim' tag, which he never much appreciated anyway. It happened because of an over-rule on the 23rd point of a magnificent second-set tie-break, which drastically affected his concentration.

At 11–11 Scottish umpire John Frame over-ruled an 'out' call that had been made on Edberg's first serve. That in itself was of little consequence. It was when Frame also decided – and television re-runs indicated correctly – that Mayotte had made his return into the net before the call and that therefore Edberg should be given the point, that the problem arose.

Mayotte was dumbfounded. He protested fiercely that the call had distracted him and he added, loudly enough for everyone to hear,

The normally busy Southfields underground station was deserted on the days of the rail strike.

Stefan Edberg had to resist two tie-breaks, the second after saving four set points, against Tim Mayotte.

Tim Mayotte's confidence was dented badly after an over-rule on the 23rd point of the second-set tie-break.

'Look, even he doesn't believe it' as he pointed to Edberg, who admitted afterwards that he would not have objected to playing a let. As tournament referee, Alan Mills, confirmed later, 'Because it was a judgement call by the umpire and not a question of fact and not a question of tennis law, neither the Referee nor the Supervisor could be called.'

Edberg actually missed a backhand top spin lob when play resumed, but followed up with a backhand crosscourt winner and a service winner to take the tie-break, in which he had saved four set points, 14–12. He went on to take the match 7–6, 7–6, 6–3.

When the tie-break finished, Mayotte, who had lost the first-set tie-break 7–2 but was still clearly in major contention until this incident happened, walked to his chair and angrily

smashed his racket on the ground. At the end of the match he offered it to Frame, saying later, 'I thought he might want it as a memento of that call.' He was also sportsmanlike enough to add, 'I shouldn't have let it get to me . . . but I did. I was disillusioned at that point. It was a big point but overall I don't think it decided the outcome.'

The prolonged wait which Edberg and Mayotte had had to endure while McEnroe was taken to 3 hours 52 minutes over a four-set victory against Mats Wilander no doubt added to the tension. Edberg even began with two double faults but on balance always seemed just to have the edge.

McEnroe's superior volleying, much of it like brilliantly effortless sword-play, evoking memories of the peaks he reached in the early 1980s, was the key to his 7–6, 3–6, 6–3, 6–4 defeat of an opponent who was left to ponder for

John McEnroe was under pressure early on against Mats Wilander.

Mats Wilander again reached the quarter-finals but then found John McEnroe too sharp and too shrewd for him once the American had recovered from losing

the first set, even if at times there was just the risk that the former champion would let things go to his head.

another year whether he will ever win Wimbledon.

A blustery wind swirling round Centre Court made returns more important than serves and, as Wilander declared afterwards, 'McEnroe is one of the best counter-punchers in the business. All I could do was hang in mentally and hope that something good would happen, because you couldn't count on a whole lot of rhythm at any stage.'

Wilander created, but too often surrendered, chances, not least after two of his most spectacular lobs helped him to three opportunities for a double service break and a 3–0 lead in the third set. Sadly, he was forced to acknowledge that on the day McEnroe had certainly been better on the big points.

It was close and tantalizing, without being truly exciting. Certainly one was never quite sure, especially when there was an exchange of service breaks in the seventh and eighth games of the fourth set, which way the match would go. In all there were 17 breaks of serve (and 53 break points) in 41 games, the last of them coming when Wilander, having saved two break points which had offered the American the chance to serve out for the match, finally volleyed a backhand beyond the baseline on the third.

Lengthy matches between McEnroe and Wilander, who had shared the honours in their previous 12 matches, are hardly uncommon. Their 6 hour 32 minute battle in 1982 remains a Davis Cup record. This one, in which McEnroe produced two of his finest among countless

Ivan Lendl takes a rest between 21 aces while his opponent, Dan Goldie, has treatment for a leg injury which eventually ruined the early strength of his quarter-final challenge.

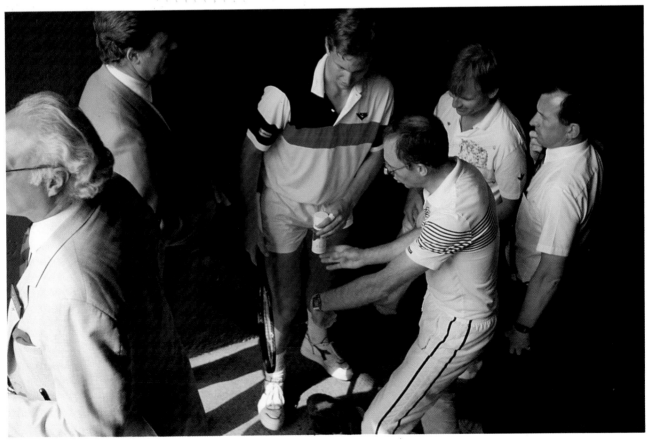

winning returns to help him break back from 0–2 in the fourth set, not only outlasted Ivan Lendl against Dan Goldie, which started at almost the same time on Court 1, but the match which followed that, Boris Becker v Paul Chamberlin, as well.

There were a number of similarities in the way Lendl and Becker advanced towards a repeat of their 1988 semi-final. Both won in straight sets against unseeded Americans, both took the final set of their matches 6–0 and both added considerably to their register of aces during the fortnight.

Lendl's tally for the afternoon was 21 but not really as impressive as it sounded, for Goldie, who had pulled a hamstring in his left leg during practice with Jeremy Bates the day before, was unable to do more than make a token effort to reach many of them. Even so he still gallantly did well enough on his own serve, in a 7–6, 7–6, 6–0 defeat, pressing Lendl to 10–8 in the first of their tie-breaks, before being willing to concede that his task was a hopeless one. No doubt the fact that he had won all seven of his earlier tie-breaks in reaching the last eight, and had won the opening set in both of his two previous encounters with the top seed, helped him ignore the increasing pain and restriction, at least until the second tie-break ran away from him 7–4.

'It was kind of depressing,' said Goldie after losing the third set in 23 minutes at a cost, to Lendl, of only seven points. 'I had the chance to play one of the biggest games of my life and I was injured.' At least he had those victories over Jimmy Connors and Slobodan Zivojinovic to remember after having drawn a blank on the first three of his Wimbledon visits.

Life on the Wimbledon campus on this particular day was no easier for the other former college boy, Chamberlin. He found former champion, Becker, in such bruising, irresistible form that at one time, fed up with having aces slammed past him or other service winners drilled into him, Chamberlin good-naturedly stopped the West German as he was about to launch into another ferocious delivery and asked, 'Which side are you going to hit this one?' Becker smiled – and hit another service winner.

It was all over in 94 minutes, 6–1, 6–2, 6–0, and Becker was understandably elated by his form, especially as he still had not dropped a set. As Chamberlin observed, 'He must have a pretty good shot at winning the tournament if he continues to play like that. I think there are three guys still in there with a chance – Boris, Stefan Edberg and John McEnroe.' Lendl would not have been pleased had he been around to hear – but he might have understood.

Meanwhile there were more surprises in the doubles, most especially the defeat of Steffi Graf and Gabriela Sabatini, defending champions in the women's doubles, as they were beaten 7–6, 6–4 in the quarter-finals by Nicole Provis and Elna Reinach, who had taken a set from them in Paris.

The match provided a fine example of how much easier so many clay-court players find it is to adapt to the demands of grass-court play in doubles than singles. Normally wild horses would find it difficult to make Miss Provis a willing volleyer; Miss Reinach's enthusiasm for the skill is not much greater; but on this occasion both volleyed with great dexterity and determination in between defending energetically when necessary.

Having taken the first-set tie-break 7–0, when Miss Graf's mind seemed to be thinking ahead to her semi-final in the singles and Miss Sabatini simply looked despondent, Miss Provis and Miss Reinach romped through the second set in 29 minutes.

Top seeds and former champions, Pam Shriver and Martina Navratilova, also struggled for a while, dropping a set to Brenda Schultz and Andrea Temesvari before squeezing through, 7–6, 6–7, 7–5. In the men's doubles, Patrick McEnroe was unable to match his brother's success. He and Jim Grabb, the fourth seeds, were surprisingly upset by Javier Frana of Argentina and Leonardo Lavalle of Mexico, two South Americans who actually enjoy playing on grass, 6–4, 6–4, 6–4.

Boris Becker's eye seldom strayed off the ball as he overwhelmed Paul Chamberlin (below left).

One fan at least was prepared for anything, rain or shine.

The way was cleared for Steffi Graf and Martina Navratilova to contest their third consecutive final. No one was totally surprised, least of all Chris Evert, who waved goodbye to the Centre Court crowd which has admired her for 18 years, and yet it was the first time that such a sequence of events would be happening at Wimbledon since 1907.

Rex Bellamy, in his last summer as the always entertaining lawn tennis correspondent of *The Times*, came up with that nugget of information and adorned it with the fact that former champions watching from the Royal Box, as the final came about, included Pauline Betz, Louise Brough and Margaret Osborne, three Americans who dominated the finals for an entire decade after the Second World War but never produced the same final three times in a row.

As matches, both semi-finals reached a predictable outcome. It was disappointing, however, that there was not more emotion and excitement in the process. Even Mrs Evert's valedictory appearance was surprisingly low-key. On this, the hottest, stickiest day of The Championships, the crowd was willing its heroine to play well. It did not expect her to win, but the groans of almost shared despair early on, when she double-faulted to lose the opening game and then missed several other inviting chances, resembled those days when Christine

Truman used to take her supporters on such emotional roller-coaster rides.

Some of the rallies were long enough to jog the memories of those who recalled Mrs Evert at her peak from 1974 – when Miss Graf, at five, was just coming to grips with her first, short-handled racket – to 1982. At least two of the rallies spanned more than 30 strokes, although Mrs Evert was honest enough later to admit, with a smile, 'I was out of breath after some of them.'

The score was 6–2, 6–1 and it lasted 68 minutes, which meant that Mrs Evert still made Miss Graf work harder than most. She was happy with that and to have justified her seeding yet again. Miss Graf did not need to do anything special. Her dominance was always evident, particularly whenever she bounced forward to drum away that imposing forehand.

Any hopes Mrs Evert held of turning the afternoon into anything more than a sentimental affair vanished when she was broken to 1–2 in the second set after one stupendous smash from Miss Graf and a host of other, increasingly extravagant shots which were the mark of a true champion.

'She's so strong and she's getting stronger all the time: she's hitting the ball harder and moving faster,' said Mrs Evert of the world and Olympic champion. 'Last year she played unbelievably but I still think you're going to see even better from her. She's probably the best I've ever seen.' As for her future, Mrs Evert continued, 'I can't see myself improving at this point. I would really be shocked if I came back and played this tournament again next year. I don't know, it would take a transplant or something.' What was she thinking about as she walked off the court, with a longer than usual glance back at the crowd? 'A whole lot of things and just that, you know, that Centre Court is the greatest court in the world. I'll always remember it.'

While Mrs Evert was happily reminiscing over a Wimbledon career which had begun in June 1972, Miss Navratilova was giving herself another chance to beat the Helen Wills Moody record with a ninth singles win, but only after overcoming an extraordinary incident after the first game of her 7–6, 6–2 victory over Catarina Lindqvist.

For many, part of the fun is being in the queues waiting to get into The All England Club grounds.

Steffi Graf made sure it would never be more than a sentimental occasion for Mrs Evert.

Having finished off the first game with an ace, she was walking away from her chair to continue the match when she suddenly stopped and appeared to be gasping for breath. Tears welled up in her eyes. It was all to do with nerves. In her anxiety she swallowed some saliva the wrong way and the next thing she knew her stomach, as she put it, was 'a mess'. It was not until six games later, by which time it was also clear that the appealing, but still wastefully erratic, Swedish player was not likely to challenge her too severely, that she felt everything had settled down again.

It was a suitable moment for Miss Navratilova to recall other disasters which had befallen her in previous years, invariably in full view of the Royal Box. 'What else can happen to me on Centre Court?' she was asking herself. 'I've been through it. I've been hit on the head by a ball, my skirt has fallen off and now here I was, all of a sudden, unable to breathe.'

For several games, the anxiety of Miss Navratilova was reflected by the untidiness of her game. Miss Lindqvist broke for 4–3 in the opening set, but the former champion came up with a glorious sliced angled backhand drop shot to earn an immediate chance to break back, which she did when her opponent was unable to return one of the few 'shooters' in a year when all the courts played so superbly.

The joy of Miss Lindqvist's backhand was more than muted by the vulnerability of her second serve, and although she rallied from 2–4 to lead 5–4, with two serves to come in the tie-break, her forehand then nervously broke down.

Miss Navratilova, who wound up her 64-minute victory with an ace, said of the final, 'I want it badly, Steffi wants it badly. It should be a great match. This is what you live for. You can't get any better than this.'

Elsewhere life continued to be uncomfortable for the defending champions in the various doubles competitions. In the men's doubles, the holders, Ken Flach and Robert Seguso, lost a first-set tie-break to the South Africans, Pieter Aldrich and Danie Visser, but eventually came through 6–7, 6–3, 6–2, 7–5 to meet John Fitzgerald and Anders Jarryd, one of the few pairs to get a taste of Centre Court in these rain-delayed Championships.

Top seeds Rick Leach and Jim Pugh did not have it any easier than the holders. They were

'Goodbye, and thanks for the memories,' says Chris Evert with what most took to be her farewell wave to the Centre Court crowd after her 17th semi-final in 18 visits to Wimbledon, before posing happily with her husband, Andy Mill, and her parents, Colette and Jimmy Evert.

Once she had settled after early lapses, Martina Navratilova was determined not to give Catarina Lindqvist any further chances to break back in their semi-final.

Fred Perry, with members of his family, cuts his 80th birthday cake, which he then sent to the ball boys and girls.

stretched over five often thrilling sets by the luckless Australians, Darren Cahill and Mark Kratzmann, before reaching the semi-finals.

Cahill and Kratzmann, both seeking compensation for their five-set near misses in the singles against John McEnroe and Miloslav Mecir respectively, played gloriously aggressive, inventive tennis to take the first and third sets, but in the end it was superior volleying by the Americans which carried them to a 3–6, 7–5, 4–6, 6–1, 6–3 success.

John McEnroe and Jakob Hlasek meanwhile were unable to continue their contest against Peter Doohan (remember him beating Boris Becker in the second round in 1987?) and fellow Australian Laurie Warder, which had been delayed from the night before. This gave rise to some alarm, happily overstated, that the American's shoulder strain might prove to be more than a minor obstacle to his chances in the singles the following day.

The major doubles upset of the day came, however, in the mixed doubles where defending champions, Zina Garrison and Sherwood Stewart, were denied any prospect of a repeat triumph when they went out in the third round to Kratzmann and another Australian, Jenny Byrne, 6–2, 6–4.

Australians Jenny Byrne and Mark Kratzmann consider their next move on their way into the mixed doubles final.

112

D A Y

11 / 12

Friday 7 July

Saturday 8 July

The second Friday was both a fascinating and infuriating day. Stefan Edberg, the defending champion and once again looking the consummate professional, reached his second successive final, as John McEnroe, in the end, went quietly.

Yet because of the light drizzle on a dull, humid, grey afternoon, which meant that for more than 200 minutes the court surface would have been too dangerous for them to continue, it was not until 7.34 pm that Edberg finally wrapped up his 7–5, 7–6, 7–6 victory. As a result, it was too late to start the second semi-final between Ivan Lendl and Boris Becker which was delayed until noon the following day, causing, as we were to discover later, even more disruption to the planned programme.

Edberg, always sharper and deeper with his volleys during a match of often high quality but modest passion, fully deserved his success against the three-times former champion, whom some had expected to produce a stronger second wind after the rain delay, especially as there had been no obvious sign of his shoulder injury.

Play, which had been scheduled for 1 pm, an hour earlier than usual because of the increasing length of men's singles semi-finals in recent years, actually started at 1.11 pm, due to the weather, and was suspended at 3.23 pm

immediately after Edberg had come to a skiddi halt, like a swan landing, as he chased a McEnr drop shot which had landed perilously close the net post.

At the time, the Swede had the first two se tucked safely away but McEnroe, who was s elated by that first-round defeat of Darren Cah from two sets down, was 3–2 ahead, on serv in the third. The opening sorties when th resumed were clearly going to be crucial ar McEnroe drew first blood with a winning servi return off the first point. However, ever time looked as if he might be creating a chance to p Edberg down, the resilient policeman's son fro Vastervik, who lives in London's Kensingto responded with something better.

There were, for instance, two consecuti brilliant top spin volley lobs which helped to g Edberg out of trouble in the eighth game of th set. McEnroe, still producing flashes of his o brilliance, but never quite enough, sens another opening when, at 5–4, he gave a clench fist salute after stepping back to launch hims into a full-blooded forehand return which su denly carried him to set point.

Edberg, unmoved by the expectations as w as excitement around the packed Centre Cou struck a perfect service winner, as if it was ju another point. Two games later he was equal resolute, when two sparrows which had bee enjoying themselves around the fringes of th court for some time suddenly landed on the n just as Edberg was about to serve at 5–6, 0–1 Once the laughter subsided, another servi winner followed.

While there was a sustained authority abo Edberg almost from first point to last, McEnroe game fluctuated, particularly his serve, which le to far more double faults than he will care remember. The last of the nine was especial damaging, for it left him 3–1 down in the third-s tie-break and, just to make matters worse, then left a backhand pass, hit late by Edber which carried just enough spin to allow it to dri in.

Although McEnroe forced two rare volleyin errors from Edberg on the next two points an another to save the first match point, it was a

Stefan Edberg took off in fine style against John McEnroe.

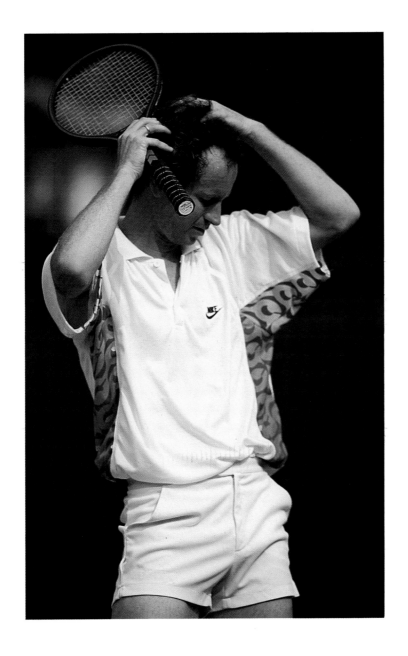

'I can't believe it,' John McEnroe seems to be saying
to himself, as he goes so close, but not quite close
enough in the semi-finals, leaving Stefan Edberg
(overleaf) to celebrate being in the final again before
the customary handshake at the end.

over moments later when Edberg's backhand swept away a somewhat wearily delivered McEnroe second serve. 'I was very happy with the way I played, I served very well,' said Edberg, whose only lapse in this respect had been in the fifth game of the opening set when, pressing a shade too much, he double-faulted twice. 'The real difference was that I hit good shots when I really needed to. It feels great to be back in the final.'

It had been a brave, often bold comeback attempt by McEnroe, who did not offer his shoulder injury as an excuse, but he was never quite the McEnroe of old, in any of his guises.

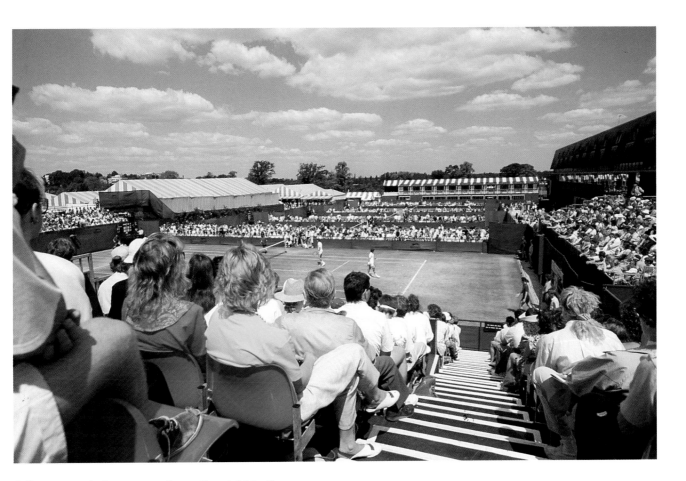

A fine general view across from Court 14 to the new Lawn Tennis Association hospitality pavilion on the far side of Court 17.

Jennifer Capriati, 13, an American tipped for future stardom, was beaten in the quarter-finals of the junior girls' singles by eventual champion, Andrea Strnadova from Czechoslovakia.

Elsewhere on this truncated day some progress was made in the doubles and some of it was highly significant, although it did little to clear the backlog of matches for some of those, such as Jim Pugh and his mixed doubles partner Jana Novotna, still involved in more than one event.

Not that either of them minded while they kept winning, and Miss Novotna, partnered by fellow Czechoslovakian Helena Sukova, knocked out the top-seeded former champions, Martina Navratilova and Pam Shriver, in the semi-finals of the women's doubles, 7–6, 7–5.

There was a three-hour rain delay in the middle of the second set when they were trailing 3–4, on serve. When they resumed the score reached 5–5 but then Miss Navratilova, not wanting to delay longer than necessary on what should have been the eve of her women's singles final, suffered a lapse of concentration which led to her losing her service to love. Miss Sukova then gleefully served out to love for a notable success.

Larissa Savchenko and Natalia Zvereva made it to the final for a second consecutive year with a 6–2, 6–2 victory over Nicole Provis and Elna Reinach, yet even so the Russian pair still had not

Ivan Lendl's celebration when he led by two sets to one was premature...

had an opportunity to play on Centre Court. The weather has a lot to answer for.

In the men's doubles Rick Leach and Jim Pugh moved into the final with a straight sets defeat of Javier Frana and Leonardo Lavalle, but John Fitzgerald and Anders Jarryd had to wait until the next day, when in fact the weather was even worse, before they were able to complete the 4–6, 6–2, 6–2, 6–3 defeat of the defending champions, Ken Flach and Robert Seguso.

The sun was shining strongly just after noon on the second Saturday when Becker and Lendl began their semi-final. When Becker, who had taken the opening set on one service break in the eleventh game, broke for 3–2 in the second, he was striding about the court with such authority and hitting his shots with such confidence that it seemed as if Steffi Graf and Martina Navratilova, due to start the women's singles final at 2 pm, would not be left kicking their heels for too long.

Becker's concentration, not for the first time, wavered, however. He lost his next service game, missed two more chances to break for 6–5 and then with the exception of two aces, played an

extraordinarily tentative tie-break which he lost 7–2. Suddenly we were back with a match which became an enthralling 4 hour 1 minute contest, which Becker might have won in straight sets but which Lendl also had within his grasp, before the West German once again ruined Lendl's never-ending dream of winning Wimbledon.

When Lendl, who was leading by two sets to one at the time, broke for 3–2 in the fourth set on a Becker double fault, the Czechoslovakian must have felt his ten years of hard labour would at least carry him into the final for the third time in the last four years. Instead, the mounting elation which he and his many supporters must have been feeling was almost instantly plunged into despair. A double fault not only allowed Becker to break back to 3–3 but inspired the 1985 and 1986 champion to launch a rousing, vigorous finish.

Lendl's heart was clearly on his sleeve in the early stages of the final set. After Becker had struck the 14th and 15th of his 17 aces to hold for 2–1, Lendl was left distraught by an over-rule which made him 0–30 in the next game. 'C'mon,'

...for Boris Becker promptly picked himself up and went on to demonstrate again why, on grass at least, he is number one.

he called to Paolo Pereira from Brazil, one of the tour's full-time umpires, 'that's the third in the last three games. I'm having a hard enough time on my own. Why do you make it even more difficult for me?' And then, with almost heart-broken resignation he added, 'Oh . . . that's unbelievable.'

For the first set and a half Becker had been in the driving seat. Lendl served well enough, but at 5–5, 40–15 he ran into trouble when the West German began a purple patch of blistering backhands which brought a swift climax to the set.

Lendl was 3–0 and two breaks ahead in the third set when what he called 'mizzle' caused a 75-minute interruption, which certainly aided his opponent more than it did him. 'The rain was definitely good for me,' said Becker, and Lendl agreed. 'Mentally they [coach Bob Brett and manager Ion Tiriac] picked him up,' he said. 'I had the feeling he [Becker] didn't know what to do before the break.' Although Lendl produced an ace on the first point after they re-started and went on to take the third set, it all began to go horribly wrong for him in that crucial sixth game of the fourth set, just when it should have been going so right. Once Becker's backhand had been given the chance to start flowing exquisitely again, Lendl's hopes slowly vanished.

Becker went on to win 7–5, 6–7, 2–6, 6–4, 6–3 . . . and within minutes the rain was back, much heavier than before. The bouquets which Miss Graf and Miss Navratilova were about to carry out on to the court for their final had to remain on their locker-room dressing tables. For the first time since 1973 the women's singles final had to be delayed until the same day as the men's final and, for the first time at least in modern years, that meant the ladies also playing on a Sunday.

D A Y

13 / 14

Sunday 9 July

Monday 10 July

For those with tickets for the final Sunday, this was the jackpot . . . two singles finals for the price of one, and although it was mostly cool and windy, there was no indication of further rain. Sir Rex Harrison, one of the guests in the Royal Box, was not the only one hoping that any more of the rain from Spain would stay mainly in the plain!

The line-up for both of the matches was exactly what most people debating rationally, rather than sentimentally, had expected: Steffi Graf v Martina Navratilova, one and two respectively in the world rankings, and Stefan Edberg v Boris Becker, not just the reigning champion against a former title-holder but undoubtedly the game's finest two players on grass courts.

It took Miss Graf just 1 hour 32 minutes to restore her supremacy, which had been temporarily brought into question by what happened in Paris four weeks earlier. A stunning ace down the middle, her fifth of the match on her first match point, completed her 6–2, 6–7, 6–1 victory and left Helen Wills Moody, eagerly following the action on television at her home in California's Monterey peninsula, still sharing the record of eight singles titles with Miss Navratilova.

Yet although the outcome was the same as in 1988, when Miss Graf ended Miss Navratilova's

six-year reign, the world champion was pressed much more intently than the challenger's earlier performances had suggested. Even though Miss Graf, leading 3–2 at the time, had held at least one point to win all of the first five games, Miss Navratilova showed no sign of nervousness in the opening set when the West German allowed her only ten points.

This was her 101st singles match at The Championships and she had gone to inordinate lengths this time to give herself every opportunity to regain the title. Fleetingly there was just the budding possibility that she might do so, when, despite being caught at 5–5 from 2–5 in the second set, Miss Navratilova went on to level the match in a 7–1 tie-break, which she played close to perfection.

Before the idea had a chance to crystalize, however, Miss Graf at last stopped making returns which were so high that they invited punishment, tightened her serve and, once she had broken for 3–1 in the third set by breaking to love, what followed fitted almost entirely into a predictable pattern.

Miss Navratilova had one more chance, with a break point in the fifth game, but she seemed in two minds about how to play the rally and in the end opted for a backhand approach, only for it to float over the baseline. The former champion, who had found Miss Graf's backhand far less of a weakness than she had probably supposed, deserved the sympathetic but appreciative reception she received, although neither her serve nor her volleying retained its former world-class sting.

The lasting impression from the match, which was kept alive by the second set, was that Miss Graf, even without excessive reliance on the forehand, deserved to be the champion and that Miss Navratilova just as clearly deserved to be in her tenth final.

Before this day, only four nations had provided the winners of both singles titles in the same year – Britain, the United States, Australia and France. Now, for West Germany, it was up to Becker. He could not have responded more magnificently. Indeed, he produced a phenomenal display of all-court power to join Fred Perry, Rod Laver, John Newcombe, Bjorn Borg and John McEnroe in

Steffi Graf again had too much consistent power for Martina Navratilova in the women's singles final.

winning the title three times or more since the abolition of The Challenge Round in 1922.

Edberg hardly knew what hit him, especially in the first set, which he lost 6–0 in 22 minutes, the first opening set completed in such a fashion since Bill Johnston overwhelmed Francis Hunter in 1923. The 1988 champion, who must have thought that the extra day's rest he had enjoyed since his semi-final might have been to his advantage, was literally blown away by an avalanche of heavy, intelligent serving, crunching volleys and explosive returns.

Having taken off like Concorde to dominate the first set and moved into overdrive again when he was suddenly under threat of losing the second, Becker won 6–0, 7–6, 6–4 in 2 hours 12 minutes. Instead of being deflated by the mental, as well as physical, effort which had been necessary to outlast Lendl the day before, Becker's adrenalin was still in full flow. The man who since 1987 had been promising that one day he would return stronger than ever to reclaim the title which, on grass, he feels should rightly be his, played even more emphatically than he had against the top seed.

When he was not sending deep booming serves, he was striking returns which gave Edberg little respite and even less chance to reinforce his claim to have the best first volley in tennis. 'I felt a little bit that I was playing uphill today,' said Edberg, with another classic piece of understatement which, nevertheless, is also part of his charm.

The most astonishing phase of this memorable Becker performance, which at times was also his personal rebuff to those who had decided that he should be seeded only three, came after his sole lapse of concentration allowed Edberg to serve for the second set at 6–5.

A net-cord winner which, unusually for him, Edberg celebrated, rather than offering the token apology, carried the London-based Swede to his first break point at 5–5 and he grabbed the chance with a perfect forehand pass. Yet having reached 40–0, and three set points, Edberg not only lost them but in all 12 of the next 13 points, as Becker then romped through the tie-break 7–1. 'I played five bad points in a row and that put him back in the match,' said Edberg, reflecting sadly on how that twelfth game slipped away, although the pace and control of Becker's returns, especially on the backhand, as they skimmed with barely anything to spare over the net, had a strong bearing on what happened too.

It was breathtaking tennis by Becker. Almost everything he touched turned to gold. Even a mis-hit smash, when Edberg was still nobly searching for some escape route in the third set, became a net cord winner.

At 4–4, Becker made his final scintillating surge. Edberg, stung by two more crushing returns, played three courageous points to recover from 0–40 to deuce, but then volleyed deep off yet another return too powerful for him to control adequately, and finally double-faulted under the relentless pressure.

Wimbledon's youngest champion, when he was 17, had certainly, at 21, come of age. Comparing his thoughts then and now, Becker said, 'The early victories were more like a fairy tale. It wasn't true really and I didn't know what I was doing. But over the last two years I have had to work much harder than ever before and so in a way I now feel much more proud.'

After striking the last of countless service winners to complete his triumph, Becker once more raised one finger high above his head – not that anyone really needed reminding that, at Wimbledon at least, he was again number one. When he reached the umpire's chair, on an impulse, he threw his racket, as a memento, to the crowd on the far side of the standing enclosure. With it went two years of frustration.

On a lesser but still highly rewarding scale, John Fitzgerald, one of the most popular Australians, was able to celebrate becoming the Wimbledon men's doubles champion at his tenth attempt. Sweden's Anders Jarryd was his sixth partner in that period, and six times Fitzgerald's hopes had been denied by the pair who eventually became the winners.

In a lively final, the ebullient Fitzgerald played the key role as he and Jarryd, whose serve was broken twice in the first set, recovered to beat the top-seeded Americans, Rick Leach and Jim Pugh, 3–6, 7–6, 6–4, 7–6. In a rousing finish, Fitzgerald and Jarryd took the third set by breaking Leach in the tenth game, and then won the fourth-set tie-break when Fitzgerald, brilliant around the net, swooped to make a triumphant interception. At the end Fitzgerald literally swept Jarryd off his feet in delighted celebration. Both players therefore completed a clean sweep of all four Grand Slam titles, though with various partners.

On their way to the final, Fitzgerald and Jarryd had won two of their earlier matches over five sets and in the first of them, against Matt Ander and Marty Davis, had won the final set 18–16, the longest of the year at The Championships.

The final of the women's doubles was disappointingly one-sided. Jana Novotna and Helena Sukova from Czechoslovakia took only 49 minutes over a 6–1, 6–2 victory which left the Russians, Larissa Savchenko and Natalia Zvereva, runners-up for the second time.

After his disappointment in the men's doubles, Leach spent much of the rest of the day trying to join his partner, Pugh, in the final of the mixed doubles. Pugh and the industrious Miss Novotna came through 6–1, 5–7, 6–4 against Robert Seguso and Lori McNeil, but Leach, in his third match of the day (not counting a quarter-final walkover in this event against Darren Cahill and Nicole Provis) went out in the semi-finals when he and Betsy Nagelsen lost 6–4, 7–6 to Mark Kratzmann and Jenny Byrne of Australia.

While the mixed doubles final was one of the matches held over until the third Monday,

Boris Becker (overleaf) stretches for this one but was mostly in aggressive control, keeping defending champion, Stefan Edberg (right), on the run.

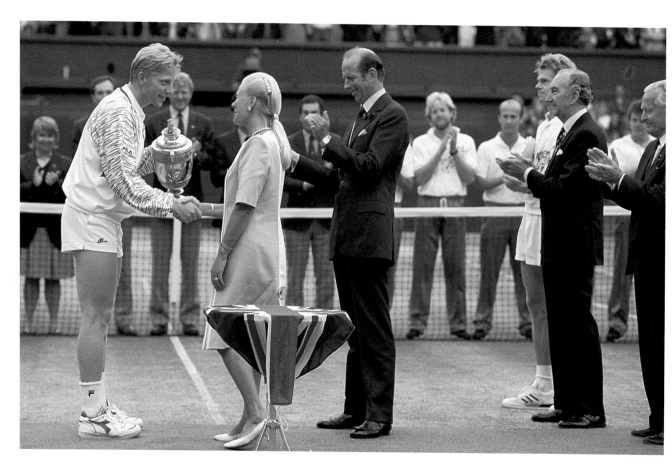

Boris Becker is congratulated by HRH The Duchess of Kent after The Duke of Kent, as President of The All England Club, had presented him with the trophy.

Wendy White beat Elna Reinach, 6–3, 6–4, to win the Ladies' Plate; and Tom Gullikson won the 35 and Over Men's Invitation Singles, beating his twin brother, Tim, for the second year in succession, 7–5, 6–3. They were thwarted in the doubles, however, losing in the semi-finals to the Amritraj brothers, Vijay and Anand, who went on to beat Dick Stockton and Bob Lutz in the final, 6–3, 6–2.

At the other end of the age scale, Niclas Kulti, a strapping young fellow with a hefty serve, and already with a world men's ranking of 183, followed Stefan Edberg in 1983 and Bjorn Borg in 1972 as winner of the boys' singles. Kulti, who did not drop a set, fully justified his top seeding when he beat the lively Australian, Todd Woodbridge, who had qualified for the main event, 6–4, 6–3, in the final.

The girls' singles title, by contrast, went to an unseeded competitor. Andrea Strnadova, from Prague, who had upset the 13-year-old American prodigy, Jennifer Capriati – fresh from her success in the junior girls' in Paris – in the quarter-finals, beat Meredith McGrath of the USA, 6–2, 6–3.

One of the real disappointments of the year

When it came to his lap of honour, Becker's hold on the trophy was not quite as secure as his grip had been on the match.

was that all the rain delays made it impossible for public and media alike to pay due attention to these supporting, but none the less often informative, events.

On the third Monday queues formed waiting for the Doherty Gates to open on a day when normally there is only clearing up to be done. This time, however, there were matches to be played on four courts, including the final of the mixed doubles on Court 1. Admission was free, and for some it was the chance of a lifetime to get at least a taste of the Wimbledon atmosphere. It was the fifth time since the 1939–45 war – the second in a row but only the tenth time in the 112-year history of The Championships – that an extra day (or more) had been necessary. Most of the 3,418 who passed through the gates, taking the total for the year to 403,706, naturally concentrated their attention on Court 1.

There, Jim Pugh, the rangy Californian, and Jana Novotna, the lively Czechoslovakian, confirmed their rating as the best mixed doubles team in the world by winning a sporting, often wonderfully resilient final from the Australians, Mark Kratzmann and Jenny Byrne, 6–4, 5–7, 6–4.

Amid plenty of enthusiasm from a crowd which included The Duchess of Kent, who went down on to the court to make the presentation, the match was decided in the early stages of the final set when Pugh and Miss Novotna took Miss Byrne's serve in the third game, during a spell when they took 14 out of 15 points.

It was the successful continuation of a partnership which had been forged by accident at the Australian Open in January 1988. Pugh, who had lost the partner he expected to play with, stopped by at the Women's International Tennis Association desk and asked them if there was anyone else who might like to partner him. Miss Novotna obliged and they promptly went on to win the title.

Their success at Wimbledon, where they saved a match point against the Americans, David Wheaton and Mary Joe Fernandez, in the quarter-finals, meant that they were then holding three of the four Grand Slam tournament mixed doubles titles. They did not play in the French.

With the sun shining again at last almost as brightly as it had done on the first Monday, the refreshment stands continued to do a roaring trade and there were plenty of picnickers on the lawns, as spectators nipped in and out of the remaining matches in the boys' and girls' doubles events, still in play.

One had to sympathize with Todd Woodbridge. He had started the final weekend with the chance of a singles and doubles twin success, and in the doubles it would have been his third consecutive triumph, for he had won the event in the two previous years with Jason Stoltenberg. This time he finished with just one runners-up award, in the singles. In the doubles he and Johan Anderson, a Swedish emigrant to Australia, went out in a tough semi-final to the South Africans, John-Laffnie De Jager and Wayne Ferreira, who in turn were beaten in the final by the more experienced young Americans, Jared Palmer and Jonathan Stark. It was decided by two tie-breaks, 7–4 and 7–2, but they had earlier traded service breaks.

The girls' doubles, which also had to complete its semi-finals before they could continue to the main business of the day, ended with what many believe will prove to have been only the first of several Wimbledon honours for Jennifer Capriati, the girl from Florida who can hardly wait to follow others such as Monica Seles into the big time. She and Meredith McGrath beat the Czechoslovakians, Andrea Strnadova and Eva Sviglerova, 6–4, 6–2, in the final.

So, a day later than planned, Wimbledon '89 drew to a pleasant, fitting close. It had been a fortnight full of fine matches and new faces. Boris Becker and Steffi Graf, almost neighbours back home in Germany, who had toasted each other at The Champions' Dinner the night before, had already left for their own extra celebrations. History will reflect their impact on tennis, already flourishing in West Germany. On a broader scale as Becker said while proudly holding the golden gleaming trophy, 'It's only when I'm a grandfather and she's a grandmother that people will realize what we have achieved!'

No one could doubt how excited John Fitzgerald (facing the camera) was when, at his tenth attempt and with his sixth different partner, he finally won the men's doubles with Anders Jarryd.

A repeat performance by Tim Gullikson (right) and brother Tom, holding the 35 and Over doubles trophy. Tom also retained his singles title.

Niclas Kulti joins an élite list of junior boys' champions, including fellow Swedes, Bjorn Borg and Stefan Edberg.

*Jim Pugh and Jana Novotna with the mixed doubles
trophy.*

*Andrea Strnadova from Czechoslovakia on her way
to winning the junior girls' title.*

CHAMPIONSHIP
RECORDS 1989

LIST OF COMPETITORS

LADIES

Adams, Miss K. M. *(U.S.A.)*
Allen, Miss L. K. *(U.S.A.)*
Amiach, Miss S. *(France)*
Antonoplis, Miss L. *(U.S.A.)*
Bakkum, Miss C. *(Netherlands)*
Balestrat, Mrs. C. M. *(Australia)*
Barg, Miss P. *(U.S.A.)*
Barnard, Miss L. *(South Africa)*
Benjamin, Miss C. *(U.S.A.)*
Bollegraf, Miss M. M. *(Netherlands)*
Borneo, Miss B. A. *(Great Britain)*
Bowes, Miss B. A. *(U.S.A.)*
Budarova, Miss I. *(Czechoslovakia)*
Bunge, Miss B. *(West Germany)*
Burgin, Miss E. M. *(U.S.A.)*
Byrne, Miss J. M. *(Australia)*
Casals, Miss R. *(U.S.A.)*
Coetzer, Miss A. J. *(South Africa)*
Collins, Miss S. L. *(U.S.A.)*
Cunningham, Miss C. E. *(U.S.A.)*
Daniels, Mrs. P. F. *(U.S.A.)*
Date, Miss K. *(Japan)*
Dechaume, Miss A. *(France)*
Demongeot, Miss I. *(France)*
Derly, Miss E. *(France)*
Devries, Miss A. *(Belgium)*
Driehuis, Miss I. *(Netherlands)*
Eldredge, Miss L. A. *(U.S.A.)*
Evert, Mrs. C. M. *(U.S.A.)*
Faber, Miss D. L. *(U.S.A.)*
Fairbank, Miss R. D. *(South Africa)*
Faull, Miss J.-A. *(Australia)*
Fendick, Miss P. A. *(U.S.A.)*
Fernandez, Miss A. M. *(U.S.A.)*
Fernandez, Miss G. *(U.S.A.)*
Fernandez, Miss M. J. *(U.S.A.)*
Ferrando, Miss L. *(Italy)*
Field, Miss L. *(Australia)*
Frazier, Miss A. *(U.S.A.)*
Fuchs, Miss J. *(U.S.A.)*
Garrison, Miss Z. L. *(U.S.A.)*
Gildemeister, Mrs. L. *(Peru)*

Golarsa, Miss L. *(Italy)*
Goles, Miss S. *(Yugoslavia)*
Gomer, Miss S. L. *(Great Britain)*
Graf, Miss S. *(West Germany)*
Graham, Miss D. *(U.S.A.)*
Gregory, Miss L. J. *(South Africa)*
Grossi, Miss M. *(Italy)*
Grossman, Miss A. *(U.S.A.)*
Grunfeld, Miss A. L. *(Great Britain)*
Guerree, Miss N. *(France)*
Hakami, Miss E. *(U.S.A.)*
Halard, Miss J. *(France)*
Hanika, Miss S. *(West Germany)*
Harper, Mrs. T. A. *(U.S.A.)*
Henricksson, Miss A. B. *(U.S.A.)*
Herr, Miss E. A. *(U.S.A.)*
Herreman, Miss N. *(France)*
Hetherington, Miss J. M. *(Canada)*
Hiraki, Miss R. *(Japan)*
Hobbs, Miss A. E. *(Great Britain)*
Holden, Miss J. *(Great Britain)*
Hy, Miss P. *(Hong Kong)*
Inoue, Miss E. *(Japan)*
Jagerman, Miss N. A. M. *(Netherlands)*
Jaggard, Miss M. *(Australia)*
Javer, Miss M. *(Great Britain)*
Kaplan, Miss J. C. *(U.S.A.)*
Kelesi, Miss H. *(Canada)*
Kessaris, Miss K. *(U.S.A.)*
Kidowaki, Miss M. *(Japan)*
Kijimuta, Miss A. *(Japan)*
Kohde-Kilsch, Miss C. *(West Germany)*
Krapl, Miss E. *(Switzerland)*
Kuczynska, Miss I. *(Poland)*
Lake, Miss V. *(Great Britain)*
Langrova, Miss P. *(Czechoslovakia)*
Lindqvist, Miss C. *(Sweden)*
Lindstrom, Miss M. *(Sweden)*
Louis, Miss J. *(Great Britain)*
Ludloff, Miss H. A. *(U.S.A.)*
MacGregor, Miss C. *(U.S.A.)*
MacGregor, Miss C. B. *(U.S.A.)*

Magers, Mrs. S. W. *(U.S.A.)*
Mandlikova, Miss H. *(Australia)*
Martin, Miss S. L. *(U.S.A.)*
McDonald, Miss K. *(Australia)*
McGrath, Miss M. *(U.S.A.)*
McNeil, Miss L. M. *(U.S.A.)*
Meier, Miss S. *(West Germany)*
Minter, Miss A. L. *(Australia)*
Miro, Miss G. *(Brazil)*
Miyagi, Miss N. *(Japan)*
Moreno, Miss P. *(Hong Kong)*
Morton, Miss T. J. *(Australia)*
Na, Miss Hu *(U.S.A.)*
Nagelsen, Miss B. *(U.S.A.)*
Navratilova, Miss M. *(U.S.A.)*
Nishiya, Miss A. *(Japan)*
Norwood, Miss M. C. *(U.S.A.)*
Novotna, Miss J. *(Czechoslovakia)*
O'Halloran, Miss L. *(Ireland)*
Okamoto, Miss K. *(Japan)*
O'Neill, Miss L. *(Australia)*
Paradis, Miss P. *(France)*
Pawlik, Miss M. *(West Germany)*
Paz, Miss M. *(Argentina)*
Pete, Mrs. M. H. *(U.S.A.)*
Pfaff, Miss E. S. *(West Germany)*
Phelps, Miss T. *(U.S.A.)*
Pollard, Miss C. *(Great Britain)*
Porwik, Miss C. *(West Germany)*
Pospisilova, Miss J. *(Czechoslovakia)*
Potter, Miss B. C. *(U.S.A.)*
Provis, Miss N. *(Australia)*
Quentrec, Miss K. *(France)*
Radford, Miss K. *(Australia)*
Rajchrtova, Miss R. *(Czechoslovakia)*
Reggi, Miss R. *(Italy)*
Reinach, Miss E. *(South Africa)*
Reis, Miss R. *(U.S.A.)*
Reynolds, Miss C. S. *(U.S.A.)*
Richardson, Miss J. A. *(New Zealand)*
Rinaldi, Miss K. S. *(U.S.A.)*
Romano, Miss B. *(Italy)*

Sabatini, Miss G. *(Argentina)*
Salmon, Miss J. A. *(Great Britain)*
Sanchez Vicario, Miss A. *(Spain)*
Savchenko, Miss L. *(U.S.S.R.)*
Scheuer-Larsen, Miss T. *(Denmark)*
Schimper, Miss K. T. *(South Africa)*
Schultz, Miss B. *(Netherlands)*
Scott, Miss A. *(U.S.A.)*
Seles, Miss M. *(Yugoslavia)*
Shriver, Miss P. H. *(U.S.A.)*
Simpkin, Miss A. *(Great Britain)*
Simpson, Miss R. K. *(Canada)*
Sloane, Miss S. P. *(U.S.A.)*
Smith, Miss S. L. *(Great Britain)*
Smoller, Miss J. *(U.S.A.)*
Smylie, Miss P. D. *(Australia)*
Sprung, Miss H. *(Austria)*
Stafford, Miss S. *(U.S.A.)*
Steinmetz, Miss K. A. *(U.S.A.)*
Strandlund, Miss M. *(Sweden)*
Suire, Miss C. *(France)*
Sukova, Miss H. *(Czechoslovakia)*
Sviglerova, Miss E. *(Czechoslovakia)*
Tanvier, Miss C. *(France)*
Tauziat, Miss N. *(France)*
Temesvari, Miss A. *(Hungary)*
Tessi, Miss C. *(Argentina)*
Thomas, Miss J. E. *(U.S.A.)*
Thompson, Miss J. G. *(Australia)*
Turnbull, Miss W. M. *(Australia)*
Van Buuren, Miss A. *(Netherlands)*
Van Nostrand, Miss M. *(U.S.A.)*
Van Rensburg, Miss D. S. *(South Africa)*
White, Miss R. M. *(U.S.A.)*
White, Miss W. E. *(U.S.A.)*
Wiesner, Mrs. H. W. *(Austria)*
Witvoet, Miss H. D. *(Netherlands)*
Wood, Miss C. J. *(Great Britain)*
Yanagi, Miss M. *(Japan)*
Zambrzycki, Miss T. *(Brazil)*
Zrubakova, Miss R. *(Czechoslovakia)*
Zvereva, Miss N. *(U.S.S.R.)*

GENTLEMEN

Acioly, R. *(Brazil)*
Agenor, R. *(Haiti)*
Aldrich, P. *(South Africa)*
Ali, Z. *(India)*
Amritraj, V. *(India)*
Anger, M. W. *(U.S.A.)*
Annacone, P. *(U.S.A.)*
Antonitsch, A. *(Austria)*
Bailey, C. A. *(Great Britain)*
Bale, L. *(Australia)*
Banducci, C. *(Italy)*
Bates, M. J. *(Great Britain)*
Bathman, R. *(Sweden)*
Baur, P. *(West Germany)*
Becker, B. *(West Germany)*
Bergh, R. *(Sweden)*
Bergstrom, C. *(Sweden)*
Birner, S. *(Czechoslovakia)*
Borwick, N. *(Australia)*
Botfield, S. *(Great Britain)*
Broad, N. *(South Africa)*
Brown, N. *(Great Britain)*
Bruguera, S. *(Spain)*
Cahill, D. *(Australia)*
Camporese, O. *(Italy)*
Campos, D. *(Brazil)*
Cancellotti, F. *(Italy)*
Cane, P. *(Italy)*
Canter, J. *(U.S.A.)*
Carbonell, T. *(Spain)*
Carlsson, J. *(Sweden)*
Castle, A. N. *(Great Britain)*
Chamberlin, P. *(U.S.A.)*
Champion, T. *(France)*
Chang, M. *(U.S.A.)*
Cherkasov, A. *(U.S.S.R.)*
Chesnokov, A. *(U.S.S.R.)*
Cihak, J. *(Czechoslovakia)*
Colombini, U. *(Italy)*
Connell, G. *(Canada)*
Connors, J. S. *(U.S.A.)*
Courier, J. *(U.S.A.)*
Curren, K. *(U.S.A.)*
Daher, J. *(Brazil)*
Davis, M. *(U.S.A.)*
Davis, S. E. *(U.S.A.)*
De la Pena, H. *(Argentina)*
Depalmer, M. *(U.S.A.)*

Deppe, R. *(South Africa)*
Devries, S. *(U.S.A.)*
Donnelly, G. W. *(U.S.A.)*
Doohan, P. *(Australia)*
Drewett, B. D. *(Australia)*
Dyke, B. *(Australia)*
Edberg, S. *(Sweden)*
Edwards, E. *(South Africa)*
Evernden, K. *(New Zealand)*
Felgate, D. C. *(Great Britain)*
Fitzgerald, J. B. *(Australia)*
Flach, K. *(U.S.A.)*
Fleurian, J. *(France)*
Flur, M. *(U.S.A.)*
Frana, J. *(Argentina)*
Fulwood, N. A. *(Great Britain)*
Furlong, S. *(Australia)*
Garnett, B. *(U.S.A.)*
Giammalva, S. *(U.S.A.)*
Gilbert, B. *(U.S.A.)*
Goldie, D. *(U.S.A.)*
Gomez, A. *(Ecuador)*
Goodall, J. M. *(Great Britain)*
Grabb, J. *(U.S.A.)*
Gunnarsson, J. *(Sweden)*
Gustafsson, M. *(Sweden)*
Herrera, L. E. *(Mexico)*
Hlasek, J. *(Switzerland)*
Hogstedt, T. *(Sweden)*
Holm, H. *(Sweden)*
Holmes, G. *(U.S.A.)*
Honey, C. *(South Africa)*
Ivanisevic, G. *(Yugoslavia)*
Jarryd, A. *(Sweden)*
Jelen, E. *(West Germany)*
Jensen, L. B. *(U.S.A.)*
Jones, K. *(U.S.A.)*
Kratzmann, M. *(Australia)*
Krickstein, A. *(U.S.A.)*
Kriek, J. C. *(U.S.A.)*
Krishnan, R. *(India)*
Kroon, N. *(Sweden)*
Kruger, S. *(South Africa)*
Kuhnen, P. *(West Germany)*
Laurendeau, M. *(Canada)*
Lavalle, L. *(Mexico)*
Layendecker, G. *(U.S.A.)*
Leach, R. *(U.S.A.)*

Lendl, I. *(Czechoslovakia)*
Letts, J. *(U.S.A.)*
Levine, B. H. *(South Africa)*
Levine, J. *(U.S.A.)*
Limberger, C. A. *(Australia)*
Lloyd, J. M. *(Great Britain)*
Lozano, J. *(Mexico)*
Luna, F. *(Spain)*
Lundgren, P. *(Sweden)*
Man Son Hing, B. *(U.S.A.)*
Mansdorf, A. *(Israel)*
Marcelino, D. *(Brazil)*
Masur, W. *(Australia)*
Matuszewski, R. *(U.S.A.)*
Mayotte, T. S. *(U.S.A.)*
McEnroe, J. P. *(U.S.A.)*
McEnroe, P. *(U.S.A.)*
Mecir, M. *(Czechoslovakia)*
Menezes, M. *(Brazil)*
Michibata, G. *(Canada)*
Mortensen, M. *(Denmark)*
Motta, C. *(Brazil)*
Muller, G. *(South Africa)*
Nargiso, D. *(Italy)*
Nastase, M. *(Rumania)*
Navratil, J. *(Czechoslovakia)*
Nijssen, T. *(Netherlands)*
Norval, P. *(South Africa)*
Novacek, K. *(Czechoslovakia)*
Page, B. *(U.S.A.)*
Palandjian, P. *(U.S.A.)*
Paloheimo, V. *(Finland)*
Pate, D. *(U.S.A.)*
Pawsat, T. *(U.S.A.)*
Pearce, B. *(U.S.A.)*
Pereira, N. *(Venezuela)*
Pernfors, M. *(Sweden)*
Petchey, M. R. J. *(Great Britain)*
Pfitzner, G. *(Australia)*
Pridham, C. *(Canada)*
Pugh, J. *(U.S.A.)*
Rahnasto, O. *(Finland)*
Raoux, J. *(France)*
Reneberg, R. A. *(U.S.A.)*
Riglewski, U. *(West Germany)*
Rive, J. *(U.S.A.)*
Robertson, M. *(South Africa)*
Roese, F. *(Brazil)*

Rostagno, D. *(U.S.A.)*
Saceanu, C. *(West Germany)*
Sampras, P. *(U.S.A.)*
Scanlon, W. *(U.S.A.)*
Schapers, M. *(Netherlands)*
Scott, L. *(U.S.A.)*
Seguso, R. *(U.S.A.)*
Shaw, S. M. *(Great Britain)*
Shelton, B. *(U.S.A.)*
Shiras, L. *(U.S.A.)*
Siegel, T. *(U.S.A.)*
Skoff, H. *(Austria)*
Smith, R. *(Bahamas)*
Srejber, M. *(Czechoslovakia)*
Steeb, C.-U. *(West Germany)*
Stewart, S. E. *(U.S.A.)*
Stich, M. *(West Germany)*
Stoltenberg, J. *(Australia)*
Strelba, M. *(Czechoslovakia)*
Suk, C. *(Czechoslovakia)*
Svantesson, T. *(Sweden)*
Svensson, J. B. *(Sweden)*
Talbot, B. *(South Africa)*
Tarango, J. *(U.S.A.)*
Turner, J. M. *(Great Britain)*
Uribe, B. *(Spain)*
Vajda, M. *(Czechoslovakia)*
Van Emburgh, G. *(U.S.A.)*
Van Rensburg, C. J. *(South Africa)*
Van't Hof, R. W. *(U.S.A.)*
Visser, D. T. *(South Africa)*
Vogel, R. *(Czechoslovakia)*
Volkov, A. *(U.S.S.R.)*
Vysand, A. *(U.S.S.R.)*
Warder, L. *(Australia)*
Warner, S. *(U.S.A.)*
Wekesa, P. *(Kenya)*
Wheaton, D. *(U.S.A.)*
Wilander, M. *(Sweden)*
Wilkison, T. *(U.S.A.)*
Willenborg, B. *(U.S.A.)*
Winogradsky, E. *(France)*
Witsken, T. *(U.S.A.)*
Woodbridge, T. *(Australia)*
Woodforde, M. *(Australia)*
Wright, P. *(Ireland)*
Youl, S. *(Australia)*
Zivojinovic, S. *(Yugoslavia)*

MAIDEN NAMES OF LADY COMPETITORS

Mrs. C. M. Balestrat—Miss D. L. Fromholtz   *Mrs. P. F. Daniels*—Miss M. L. Piatek

Mrs. C. M. Evert—Miss C. M. Evert   *Mrs. L. Gildemeister*—Miss L. Arraya   *Mrs. T. A. Harper*—Miss M. Louie

Mrs. S. W. Magers—Miss G. A. Rush   *Mrs. M. H. Pete*—Miss S. A. Walsh   *Mrs. P. D. Smylie*—Miss E. M. Sayers   *Mrs. H. W. Wiesner*—Miss J. Polzl

EVENT I.—THE GENTLEMEN'S SINGLES CHAMPIONSHIP

Holder: S. EDBERG

The Winner will become the holder, for the year only, of the CHALLENGE CUP presented to the Club by KING GEORGE V, and also of the CHALLENGE CUP presented by The All England Lawn Tennis and Croquet Club. The First Prize is a piece of silver, known as "The Renshaw Cup" annually presented to the Club by the surviving members of the family of the late ERNEST and WILLIAM RENSHAW. The Winner will receive silver replicas of the two Challenge Cups. A personal prize and a Silver Medal will be presented to the Runner-up and a Bronze Medal to each defeated Semi-finalist.

FIRST ROUND

1	I. Lendl ①	(CSK)
2	N. Pereira	(VEN)
(Q) 3	B. Garnett	(USA)
(Q) 4	R. Bathman	(SWE)
5	M. Vajda	(CSK)
6	G. Michibata	(CAN)
7	T. Carbonell	(ESP)
8	M. Davis	(USA)
9	G. Ivanisevic	(YUG)
10	T. Champion	(FRA)
(W) 11	K. Flach	(USA)
(Q) 12	S. Giammalva	(USA)
13	R. Krishnan	(IND)
14	P. Lundgren	(SWE)
15	M. Stich	(DEU)
16	M. Pernfors ⑮	(SWE)
17	J. S. Connors ⑩	(USA)
18	A. Cherkasov	(SUN)
19	K. Evernden	(NZL)
20	D. Goldie	(USA)
(Q) 21	J. Rive	(USA)
(L) 22	M. W. Anger	(USA)
(Q) 23	Z. Ali	(IND)
24	W. Masur	(AUS)
25	S. Zivojinovic	(YUG)
26	A. Jarryd	(SWE)
27	J. Cihak	(CSK)
(W) 28	C. A. Bailey	(GBR)
29	M. Kratzmann	(AUS)
30	V. Paloheimo	(FIN)
(Q) 31	S. Warner	(USA)
32	M. Mecir ⑦	(CSK)
33	B. Becker ③	(DEU)
(Q) 34	B. Shelton	(USA)
35	O. Rahnasto	(FIN)
36	R. Matuszewski	(USA)
37	D. Nargiso	(ITA)
38	J. Gunnarsson	(SWE)
39	D. Rostagno	(USA)
40	S. Youl	(AUS)
41	M. Strelba	(CSK)
42	P. Kuhnen	(DEU)
43	R. Smith	(BHS)
44	P. Aldrich	(ZAF)
45	J. Frana	(ARG)
46	J. Grabb	(USA)
47	F. Cancellotti	(ITA)
48	A. Krickstein ⑬	(USA)
49	K. Curren ⑫	(USA)
(W) 50	A. N. Castle	(GBR)
(Q) 51	K. Jones	(USA)
52	M. Srejber	(CSK)
53	J. C. Kriek	(USA)
54	L. Shiras	(USA)
(W) 55	M. J. Bates	(GBR)
56	C. Motta	(BRA)
57	F. Luna	(ESP)
(W) 58	M. R. J. Petchey	(GBR)
59	J. Canter	(USA)
(Q) 60	N. A. Fulwood	(GBR)
61	P. Chamberlin	(USA)
62	G. Muller	(ZAF)
63	T. Hogstedt	(SWE)
64	J. Hlasek ⑥	(CHE)
65	J. P. McEnroe ⑤	(USA)
66	D. Cahill	(AUS)
67	R. A. Reneberg	(USA)
68	C. Saceanu	(DEU)
69	J. Courier	(USA)
70	R. Seguso	(USA)
71	J. Pugh	(USA)
72	J. Tarango	(USA)
73	J. B. Svensson	(SWE)
74	D. Wheaton	(USA)
75	P. Norval	(ZAF)
76	C. A. Limberger	(AUS)
77	G. Layendecker	(USA)
78	H. De la Pena	(ARG)
79	J. B. Fitzgerald	(AUS)
80	B. Gilbert ⑪	(USA)
81	A. Chesnokov ⑭	(SUN)
82	B. D. Drewett	(AUS)
(Q) 83	P. Baur	(DEU)
84	T. Wilkison	(USA)
85	J. Lozano	(MEX)
(Q) 86	M. Laurendeau	(CAN)
87	M. Woodforde	(AUS)
88	C. J. Van Rensburg	(ZAF)
89	J. Stoltenberg	(AUS)
(W) 90	S. Botfield	(GBR)
91	O. Camporese	(ITA)
92	C. Bergstrom	(SWE)
(W) 93	J. M. Turner	(GBR)
94	K. Novacek	(CSK)
95	M. Gustafsson	(SWE)
96	M. Wilander ④	(SWE)
97	T. S. Mayotte ⑧	(USA)
98	P. Cane	(ITA)
(Q) 99	H. Holm	(SWE)
100	N. Broad	(ZAF)
101	P. Annacone	(USA)
102	D. Pate	(USA)
103	T. Nijssen	(NLD)
104	H. Skoff	(AUT)
105	L. Lavalle	(MEX)
106	A. Gomez	(ECU)
(Q) 107	M. Robertson	(ZAF)
108	M. Schapers	(NLD)
109	R. Agenor	(HTI)
110	J. Fleurian	(FRA)
(Q) 111	W. Scanlon	(USA)
112	M. Chang ⑨	(USA)
113	A. Mansdorf ⑯	(ISR)
114	S. Bruguera	(ESP)
115	A. Volkov	(SUN)
116	E. Jelen	(DEU)
(W) 117	N. Brown	(GBR)
(Q) 118	G. Holmes	(USA)
119	T. Witsken	(USA)
120	J. Carlsson	(SWE)
121	S. E. Davis	(USA)
122	A. Vysand	(SUN)
123	D. T. Visser	(ZAF)
124	C. U. Steeb	(DEU)
125	P. Sampras	(USA)
(Q) 126	T. Woodbridge	(AUS)
127	C. Pridham	(CAN)
128	S. Edberg ②	(SWE)

SECOND ROUND

- I. Lendl ① 7-6, 4-6, 6-3, 6-7, 6-1
- R. Bathman 6-2, 6-4, 6-7, 4-6, 6-1
- M. Vajda 6-7, 6-1, 7-6, 6-3
- T. Carbonell 6-4, 3-6, 7-6, 6-4
- G. Ivanisevic 6-3, 6-4, 3-6, 6-3
- K. Flach 7-6, 7-6, 3-6, 0-6, 6-3
- P. Lundgren 6-4, 7-6, 7-5
- M. Pernfors ⑮ 5-7, 6-1, 6-3, 6-2
- J. S. Connors ⑩ 6-3, 6-2, 4-6, 6-3
- D. Goldie 7-6, 7-6, 3-6, 6-0
- J. Rive 7-6, 6-2, 6-7, 7-5
- W. Masur 6-3, 6-4, 6-2
- S. Zivojinovic 3-6, 7-6, 6-3, 6-0
- C. A. Bailey 7-5, 6-7, 3-6, 6-3, 6-4
- M. Kratzmann 6-2, 7-6, 6-1
- M. Mecir ⑦ 6-7, 4-6, 6-1, 7-5, 7-5
- B. Becker ③ 6-1, 6-4, 7-6
- R. Matuszewski 2-6, 6-2, 6-4, 6-4
- J. Gunnarsson 3-6, 6-3, 6-7, 6-3, 6-4
- D. Rostagno 7-6, 6-4, 6-4
- P. Kuhnen 7-6, 6-2, 6-3
- P. Aldrich 7-6, 6-2, 6-4
- J. Frana 6-7, 6-3, 7-6, 5-7, 7-4
- A. Krickstein ⑬ 6-1, 6-2, 3-6, 6-1
- K. Curren ⑫ 6-2, 4-6, 7-6, 6-3
- M. Srejber 6-3, 6-3, 6-3
- L. Shiras 7-6, 6-2, 6-2
- M. J. Bates 6-7, 6-1, 4-6, 7-6, 6-3
- M. R. J. Petchey 6-2, 6-7, 6-2, 6-1
- N. A. Fulwood 7-6, 3-6, 7-6, 7-6
- P. Chamberlin 4-6, 6-3, 7-5, 6-3
- T. Hogstedt 6-3, 7-6, 6-1
- J. P. McEnroe ⑤ 4-6, 4-6, 6-2, 6-3, 8-6
- R. A. Reneberg 6-4, 6-4, 4-6, 4-6, 6-2
- R. Seguso 6-2, 3-6, 6-4, 5-7, 9-7
- J. Pugh 3-6, 6-3, 6-1, 6-3
- J. B. Svensson 7-6, 7-6, 7-6
- C. A. Limberger 7-6, 6-4, 3-6, 6-3
- G. Layendecker 6-3, 7-6, 6-0
- J. B. Fitzgerald 6-2, 7-5, 1-6, 3-6, 6-2
- B. D. Drewett 6-4, 7-6, 6-0
- T. Wilkison 6-2, 6-2, 3-6, 3-6, 6-1
- M. Laurendeau
- C. J. Van Rensburg 7-6, 6-1, 6-4
- J. Stoltenberg 7-6, 7-6, 6-3
- O. Camporese 6-3, 6-4, 6-4
- K. Novacek 1-6, 6-3, 3-6, 6-1, 6-2
- M. Wilander ④ 6-2, 6-2, 6-2
- T. S. Mayotte ⑧ 7-6, 6-0, 6-1
- H. Holm 6-1, 6-1, 6-1
- D. Pate 3-6, 7-6, 4-6, 7-5, 6-4
- T. Nijssen 7-5, 6-3, 6-2
- A. Gomez 3-6, 6-4, 6-4, 7-6
- M. Schapers 7-5, 4-6, 7-6, 6-4
- R. Agenor 4-6, 6-3, 6-3, 6-4
- M. Chang ⑨ 6-4, 6-3, 2-6, 6-3
- A. Mansdorf ⑯ 6-2, 6-1, 6-4
- E. Jelen 7-5, 6-7, 6-3, 6-2
- G. Holmes 6-3, 7-6, 6-3
- T. Witsken 6-3, 6-4, 7-6
- S. E. Davis 6-4, 1-6, 6-4, 6-4
- C. U. Steeb 7-6, 6-7, 6-3, 7-6
- T. Woodbridge 7-5, 7-6, 5-7, 6-3
- S. Edberg ② 6-3, 6-4, 6-1

THIRD ROUND

- I. Lendl ① 6-7, 6-3, 6-2, 6-2
- T. Carbonell 6-2, 6-4, 7-5
- K. Flach 6-4, 6-3, 4-6, 6-3
- P. Lundgren 7-6, 6-2, 6-4
- D. Goldie 7-6, 5-7, 6-4, 6-2
- W. Masur 6-3, 7-6, 4-6, 6-2
- S. Zivojinovic 6-3, 7-5, 7-6
- M. Mecir ⑦ 6-7, 4-6, 6-1, 7-5, 7-5
- B. Becker ③ 6-3, 7-5, 6-4
- J. Gunnarsson 6-7, 2-6, 7-5, 7-6, 9-7
- P. Kuhnen 6-1, 7-5, 6-0
- A. Krickstein ⑬ 4-6, 6-3, 3-6, 7-6, 7-5
- K. Curren ⑫ 4-6, 6-2, 6-3, 6-0
- L. Shiras 4-6, 7-5, 6-3, 6-2
- N. A. Fulwood 7-5, 6-1, 6-2
- P. Chamberlin 6-3, 6-2, 6-2
- J. P. McEnroe ⑤ 6-3, 3-6, 6-3, 7-5
- J. Pugh 6-3, 7-6, 6-3
- J. B. Svensson 6-4, 6-3, 7-6
- J. B. Fitzgerald 4-6, 6-3, 3-6, 6-3, 6-4
- B. D. Drewett 6-7, 6-3, 7-5, 6-2
- C. J. Van Rensburg 3-6, 7-6, 6-2, 6-2
- J. Stoltenberg 7-5, 6-7, 6-2, 1-6, 6-3
- M. Wilander ④ 6-3, 6-0, 6-3
- T. S. Mayotte ⑧ 7-6, 6-2, 4-6, 6-1
- D. Pate 6-4, 2-6, 1-6, 7-6, 15-13
- M. Schapers 2-6, 7-6, 7-5, 3-6, 6-3
- M. Chang ⑨ 4-6, 6-2, 6-1, 7-5
- A. Mansdorf ⑯ 6-3, 6-3, 6-3, 6-2
- G. Holmes 5-7, 6-4, 7-6, 4-6, 14-12
- S. E. Davis 7-5, 4-6, 4-6, 6-2, 6-4
- S. Edberg ② 6-4, 6-4, 1-6, 7-6

FOURTH ROUND

- I. Lendl ① 7-6, 6-3, 6-1
- P. Lundgren 6-3, 6-2, 6-7, 6-3
- D. Goldie 7-6, 7-6, 3-6, 7-6
- S. Zivojinovic 6-7, 6-1, 7-5, 6-3
- B. Becker ③ 7-5, 7-6, 6-3
- A. Krickstein ⑬ 4-6, 6-3, 6-3, 6-2
- L. Shiras 4-6, 6-3, 5-7, 7-6, 6-3
- P. Chamberlin 3-6, 7-6, 6-4, 6-2
- J. P. McEnroe ⑤ 6-3, 6-4, 6-2
- J. B. Fitzgerald 6-4, 6-4, 7-6
- C. J. Van Rensburg 6-3, 2-6, 2-6, 6-2, 10-8
- M. Wilander ④ 6-3, 6-3, 6-3
- T. S. Mayotte ⑧ 6-4, 6-1, 6-3
- M. Chang ⑨ 4-6, 6-3, 7-5, 7-5
- A. Mansdorf ⑯ 6-2, 6-4, 6-2
- S. Edberg ② 6-3, 6-4, 4-6, 6-2

QUARTER-FINALS

- I. Lendl ① 1-6, 7-6 (7-5), 6-2, 6-4
- D. Goldie 6-4, 6-4, 7-6 (8-6)
- B. Becker ③ 6-4, 6-4, 7-5
- P. Chamberlin 7-5, 6-4, 7-6 (7-4)
- J. P. McEnroe ⑤ 6-3, 6-4, 6-4
- M. Wilander ④ 3-6, 7-5, 7-5, 6-3
- T. S. Mayotte ⑧ 6-3, 6-1, 6-3
- S. Edberg ② 6-4, 6-3, 6-2

SEMI-FINALS

- I. Lendl ① 7-6 (10-8), 7-6 (7-4), 6-0
- B. Becker ③ 6-1, 6-2, 6-0
- J. P. McEnroe ⑤ 7-6 (8-6), 3-6, 6-3, 6-4
- S. Edberg ② 7-6 (14-12), 6-3, 6-3

FINAL

- B. Becker ③ 7-5, 6-7 (2-7), 2-6, 6-4, 6-3
- S. Edberg ② 7-6 (7-2), 7-6 (7-5)

WINNER

B. Becker ③ 6-0, 7-6 (7-1), 6-4

Heavy type denotes seeded players. The encircled figure against names denotes the order in which they have been seeded. (W) = Wild card. (Q) = Qualifier. (L) = Lucky loser. The Matches will be the best of five sets.

EVENT II.—THE GENTLEMEN'S DOUBLES CHAMPIONSHIP — Holders: K. FLACH and R. SEGUSO

The Winners will become the holders, for the year only, of the CHALLENGE CUPS, presented by the OXFORD UNIVERSITY LAWN TENNIS CLUB and the late SIR HERBERT WILBERFORCE respectively. The Winners will receive silver replicas of the Challenge Cups. A personal prize and a Silver Medal will be presented to each of the Runners-up, and a Bronze Medal to each defeated Semi-finalist.

FIRST ROUND

1. R. Leach and J. Pugh ①
2. C. Saceanu and M. Srejber
3. J. Gunnarsson and N. Kroon
(W) 4. N. Brown and N. A. Fulwood
5. S. Devries and R. Matuszewski
6. J. Cihak and C. Suk
7. R. Smith and P. Wekesa
8. J. Courier and P. Sampras ⑮
9. D. Cahill and M. Kratzmann ⑨
10. L. E. Herrera and B. Uribe
11. D. Marcelino and M. Menezes
12. P. Cane and U. Colombini
13. J. Navratil and K. Novacek
14. G. Ivanisevic and N. Pereira
15. K. Evernden and J. C. Kriek
16. K. Lozano and T. Witsken ⑫
17. J. Grabb and P. McEnroe ④
18. U. Riglewski and T. Svantesson
(Q) 19. J. Daher and F. Roese
20. E. Edwards and G. Holmes
(Q) 21. L. Bale and M. Nastase
22. J. Frana and L. Lavalle
23. J. Letts and B. Man Son Hing
24. E. Jelen and M. Mortensen ⑬
25. P. Doohan and L. Warder ⑫
26. J. Levine and T. Siegel
(Q) 27. B. Page and S. Warner
(W) 28. V. Amritraj and C. A. Bailey
29. M. Schapers and M. Stich
30. M. Depalmer and G. W. Donnelly
31. A. Antonitsch and P. Baur
32. J. Hlasek and J. P. McEnroe ⑤
33. P. Annacone and C. J. Van Rensburg ⑥
(W) 34. S. Botfield and J. M. Turner
35. G. Van Emburgh and S. Youl
36. R. Bergh and B. Pearce
37. N. Broad and S. Kruger
38. K. Jones and T. Pawsat
39. B. Gilbert and G. Muller
40. S. E. Davis and T. Wilkison ⑪
41. G. Connell and G. Michibata ⑭
42. S. Giammalva and G. Layendecker
43. O. Camporese and D. Nargiso
44. C. Motta and B. Willenborg
45. R. Acioly and D. Campos
(W) 46. J. M. Lloyd and S. M. Shaw
47. M. W. Anger and M. Davis
48. J. B. Fitzgerald and A. Jarryd ③
49. K. Curren and D. Pate ⑦
50. M. Flur and J. Rive
51. M. J. Bates and P. Lundgren
(Q) 52. Z. Ali and J. Canter
53. S. Birner and R. Vogel
54. B. Dyke and T. Nijssen
55. R. Bathman and T. Carbonell
56. P. Aldrich and D. T. Visser ⑩
57. B. D. Drewett and W. Masur ⑯
(W) 58. D. C. Felgate and J. M. Goodall
59. P. Kuhnen and C.-U. Steeb
(Q) 60. G. Raoux and E. Winogradsky
61. M. Mecir and M. Woodforde
62. M. Gustafsson and O. Rahnasto
63. A. N. Castle and R. W. Van't Hof
64. K. Flach and R. Seguso ②

SECOND ROUND

- R. Leach and J. Pugh ① — 7–6, 6–2, 6–4
- N. Brown and N. A. Fulwood — 6–4, 6–2, 6–2
- J. Cihak and C. Suk — 1–6, 6–3, 7–5, 6–7, 6–3
- J. Courier and P. Sampras ⑮ — 6–4, 6–4, 7–6
- D. Cahill and M. Kratzmann ⑨ — 6–3, 6–4, 6–3
- D. Marcelino and M. Menezes — 6–2, 6–7, 6–3, 7–6
- G. Ivanisevic and N. Pereira — 6–3, 6–3, 6–4
- K. Evernden and J. C. Kriek — 6–4, 6–2, 7–5
- J. Grabb and P. McEnroe ④ — 2–6, 6–2, 3–6, 7–6, 7–5
- J. Daher and F. Roese — 6–4, 6–4, 6–4
- J. Frana and L. Lavalle — 6–4, 7–5, 7–6
- J. Letts and B. Man Son Hing — 6–2, 2–6, 6–4, 6–4
- P. Doohan and L. Warder ⑫ — 6–3, 6–1, 6–1
- V. Amritraj and C. A. Bailey — 6–3, 6–2, 7–6
- M. Depalmer and G. W. Donnelly — 6–3, 6–4, 7–6
- J. Hlasek and J. P. McEnroe ⑤ — 6–3, 3–6, 4–6, 6–3, 6–3
- S. Botfield and J. M. Turner — 7–5, 6–3, 7–5
- G. Van Emburgh and S. Youl — 7–6, 6–3, 6–4
- N. Broad and S. Kruger — 6–4, 6–4, 6–7, 6–3
- S. E. Davis and T. Wilkison ⑪ — 6–7, 7–6, 4–6, 6–3, 6–2
- S. Giammalva and G. Layendecker — 6–3, 6–4, 3–6, 6–3
- O. Camporese and D. Nargiso — 6–7, 7–6, 7–6, 7–6
- J. M. Lloyd and S. M. Shaw — 6–1, 6–7, 6–2, 6–4
- J. B. Fitzgerald and A. Jarryd ③ — 6–7, 6–4, 6–4, 4–6, 18–16
- K. Curren and D. Pate ⑦ — 7–6, 7–6, 3–6, 6–1
- Z. Ali and J. Canter — 7–6, 3–6, 6–1, 6–7, 10–8
- B. Dyke and T. Nijssen — 6–2, 7–5, 6–2
- P. Aldrich and D. T. Visser ⑩ — 6–3, 6–4, 6–1
- B. D. Drewett and W. Masur ⑯ — 6–1, 6–3, 6–2
- G. Raoux and E. Winogradsky — 6–3, 7–6, 6–3
- M. Mecir and M. Woodforde — 5–7, 6–4, 6–4, 7–6
- K. Flach and R. Seguso ② — 3–6, 7–6, 6–4, 6–3

THIRD ROUND

- R. Leach and J. Pugh ① — 6–1, 7–5, 6–4
- J. Courier and P. Sampras — 6–3, 4–6, 7–6, 6–1
- D. Cahill and M. Kratzmann ⑨ — 6–3, 6–4, 6–2
- G. Ivanisevic and N. Pereira — 7–5, 2–6, 6–3, 7–6
- J. Grabb and P. McEnroe ④ — 6–3, 6–7, 6–4, 6–1
- J. Frana and L. Lavalle — 6–4, 6–4, 7–6
- P. Doohan and L. Warder ⑫ — 7–5, 6–1, 7–6
- J. Hlasek and J. P. McEnroe ⑤ — 6–7, 6–4, 7–5, 10–8
- G. Van Emburgh and S. Youl — 7–6, 6–3, 6–4
- N. Broad and S. Kruger — 7–5, 6–2, 6–3
- S. Giammalva and G. Layendecker — 6–3, 6–2, 6–4
- J. B. Fitzgerald and A. Jarryd ③ — w/o
- K. Curren and D. Pate ⑦ — 6–3, 3–6, 6–3, 7–6
- P. Aldrich and D. T. Visser ⑩ — 6–7, 7–6, 6–3
- G. Raoux and E. Winogradsky — 6–2, 6–4, 1–6, 2–6, 6–3
- K. Flach and R. Seguso ② — 3–6, 6–7, 6–3, 6–4, 8–6

QUARTER-FINALS

- R. Leach and J. Pugh ① — 7–6 (7–3), 6–3, 6–4
- D. Cahill and M. Kratzmann ⑨ — 6–3, 7–6 (8–6), 6–1
- J. Frana and L. Lavalle — 6–4, 6–4, 6–4
- P. Doohan and L. Warder ⑫ — 3–6, 6–4, 4–6, 4–2, Ret'd
- G. Van Emburgh and S. Youl — 7–6 (7–2), 6–4, 6–2
- J. B. Fitzgerald and A. Jarryd ③ — 2–6, 6–4, 6–4, 3–6, 6–3
- P. Aldrich and D. T. Visser ⑩ — 6–7 (8–10), 6–7 (4–7), 7–6 (12–10), 7–6 (7–4), 6–2
- K. Flach and R. Seguso ② — 6–7 (3–7), 6–2, 3–6, 6–3, 6–4

SEMI-FINALS

- R. Leach and J. Pugh ① — 3–6, 6–7, 5, 4–6, 6–1, 6–3
- J. Frana and L. Lavalle — 7–6 (7–2), 7–6 (7–5), 3–6, 6–3
- J. B. Fitzgerald and A. Jarryd ③ — 7–6 (7–5), 6–3, 6–2, 6–3
- K. Flach and R. Seguso ② — 6–7 (5–7), 6–3, 6–2, 7–5

FINAL

- R. Leach and J. Pugh ① — 6–3, 6–4
- J. B. Fitzgerald and A. Jarryd ③ — 4–6, 6–2, 6–2, 6–3

WINNER

J. B. Fitzgerald and A. Jarryd ③ — 3–6, 7–6 (7–4), 6–4, 7–6 (7–4)

Heavy type denotes seeded players. The encircled figure against names denotes the order in which they have been seeded. (W) = Wild card. (Q) = Qualifier. (L) = Lucky loser. The Matches will be the best of five sets.

146

EVENT III.—THE LADIES' SINGLES CHAMPIONSHIP

Holder: Miss S. GRAF

The Winner will become the holder, for the year only, of the CHALLENGE TROPHY presented by The All England Lawn Tennis and Croquet Club. The Winner will receive a silver replica of the Trophy. A personal prize and a Silver Medal will be presented to the Runner-up and a Bronze Medal to each defeated Semi-finalist.

FIRST ROUND

1	**Miss S. Graf ①**	(DEU)
(W) 2	Miss J. A. Salmon	(GBR)
3	Miss K. Kessaris	(USA)
4	Miss N. Herreman	(FRA)
5	Miss K. Quentrec	(FRA)
6	Miss S. Hanika	(DEU)
7	Miss A. L. Minter	(AUS)
8	Miss M. Van Nostrand	(USA)
9	Miss T. Phelps	(USA)
10	Miss I. Kuczynska	(POL)
11	Miss E. Sviglerova	(CSK)
12	Miss H. A. Ludloff	(USA)
13	Miss C. Porwik	(DEU)
14	Miss E. A. Herr	(USA)
15	Miss B. Schultz	(NLD)
16	**Miss M. Seles ⑪**	(YUG)
17	**Miss L. M. McNeil ⑮**	(USA)
18	Miss N. A. M. Jagerman	(NLD)
19	Miss B. A. Bowes	(USA)
20	Miss M. Pawlik	(DEU)
21	Miss P. Paradis	(FRA)
(W) 22	Miss W. M. Turnbull	(AUS)
23	Miss A. Grossman	(USA)
24	Mrs. H. W. Wiesner	(AUT)
(W) 25	Miss A. L. Grunfeld	(GBR)
(Q) 26	Miss S. Amiach	(FRA)
27	Miss R. Reggi	(ITA)
28	Miss P. Langrova	(CSK)
29	Miss J. Halard	(FRA)
30	Miss R. Rajchrtova	(CSK)
31	Miss J. Pospisilova	(CSK)
32	**Miss A. Sanchez Vicario ⑦**	(ESP)
33	**Mrs. C. M. Evert ④**	(USA)
34	Miss T. A. Harper	(USA)
35	Miss M. McGrath	(USA)
36	Miss Hu Na	(USA)
(Q) 37	Miss M. Jaggard	(AUS)
(W) 38	Miss A. E. Hobbs	(GBR)
39	Miss E. Reinach	(ZAF)
(L) 40	Miss G. Miro	(BRA)
(Q) 41	Miss T. J. Morton	(AUS)
(W) 42	Miss C. J. Wood	(GBR)
43	Miss P. A. Fendick	(USA)
(Q) 44	Miss J. Smoller	(USA)
45	Miss G. Fernandez	(USA)
46	Miss A. Devries	(BEL)
47	Miss S. Stafford	(USA)
48	**Miss H. Kelesi ⑬**	(CAN)
49	**Miss J. Novotna ⑩**	(CSK)
50	Miss R. K. Simpson	(CAN)
51	Miss E. M. Burgin	(USA)
52	Miss E. Hakami	(USA)
(L) 53	Miss D. Graham	(USA)
54	Miss C. E. Cunningham	(USA)
55	Miss K. M. Adams	(USA)
56	Miss A. J. Coetzer	(ZAF)
57	Miss L. Golarsa	(ITA)
58	Miss M. Paz	(ARG)
59	Miss B. Nagelsen	(USA)
60	Miss M. Strandlund	(SWE)
61	Miss L. Ferrando	(ITA)
62	Miss L. Field	(AUS)
(Q) 63	Miss K. Date	(JPN)
64	**Miss Z. L. Garrison ⑤**	(USA)
65	**Miss H. Sukova ⑥**	(CSK)
66	Miss M. Javer	(GBR)
67	Miss D. S. Van Rensburg	(ZAF)
68	Miss E. Krapl	(CHE)
69	Miss A. B. Henricksson	(USA)
70	Miss S. L. Martin	(USA)
71	Miss C. Kohde-Kilsch	(DEU)
72	Miss N. Tauziat	(FRA)
73	Miss I. Demongeot	(FRA)
74	Miss N. Guerree	(FRA)
75	Miss C. MacGregor	(USA)
76	Miss C. Lindqvist	(SWE)
77	Miss E. S. Pfaff	(DEU)
78	Miss W. E. White	(USA)
79	Miss R. Reis	(USA)
80	**Miss N. Zvereva ⑨**	(SUN)
81	**Miss M. J. Fernandez ⑫**	(USA)
82	Mrs. P. F. Daniels	(USA)
83	Miss S. Meier	(DEU)
84	Miss L. K. Allen	(USA)
85	Miss A. Nishiya	(JPN)
86	Miss C. Tanvier	(FRA)
87	Miss A. Frazier	(USA)
(W) 88	Miss A. Simpkin	(GBR)
89	Miss T. Scheuer-Larsen	(DNK)
90	Miss M. Yanagi	(JPN)
91	Mrs. P. D. Smylie	(AUS)
92	Miss J. M. Byrne	(AUS)
93	Miss R. D. Fairbank	(ZAF)
94	Miss J. A. Richardson	(NZL)
95	Mrs. C. M. Balestrat	(AUS)
96	**Miss G. Sabatini ③**	(ARG)
97	**Miss P. H. Shriver ⑧**	(USA)
(Q) 98	Miss C. Bakkum	(NLD)
99	Miss L. Eldredge	(USA)
100	Miss S. L. Gomer	(GBR)
(W)101	Miss V. Lake	(GBR)
102	Miss S. Goles	(YUG)
103	Miss M. M. Bollegraf	(NLD)
104	Mrs. S. W. Magers	(USA)
105	Miss I. Budarova	(CSK)
106	Miss K. Okamoto	(JPN)
107	Miss K. S. Rinaldi	(USA)
108	Miss J.-A. Faull	(AUS)
(W)109	Miss S. L. Smith	(GBR)
110	Mrs. L. Gildemeister	(PER)
(Q)111	Miss S. L. Collins	(USA)
112	**Miss S. P. Sloane ⑯**	(USA)
113	**Miss H. Mandlikova ⑭**	(AUS)
114	Miss R. Zrubakova	(CSK)
(L)115	Miss C. Suire	(FRA)
116	Miss A. Kijimuta	(JPN)
117	Miss D. L. Faber	(USA)
118	Miss L. Savchenko	(SUN)
119	Miss J. G. Thompson	(AUS)
120	Miss K. T. Schimper	(ZAF)
121	Miss N. Provis	(AUS)
122	Miss C. Benjamin	(USA)
123	Miss R. M. White	(USA)
124	Miss E. Inoue	(JPN)
125	Miss A. Temesvari	(HUN)
(Q)126	Miss K. Radford	(AUS)
127	Miss J. M. Hetherington	(CAN)
128	**Miss M. Navratilova ②**	(USA)

SECOND ROUND

- Miss S. Graf ① — 6-1, 6-2
- Miss K. Kessaris — 1-6, 6-4, 6-3
- Miss K. Quentrec — 6-4, 6-2
- Miss A. L. Minter — 6-0, 6-0
- Miss T. Phelps — 3-6, 6-4, 6-3
- Miss E. Sviglerova — 6-3, 6-2
- Miss C. Porwik — 4-6, 6-4, 6-3
- Miss M. Seles ⑪ — 7-6, 1-6, 6-4
- Miss L. M. McNeil ⑮ — 6-3, 6-1
- Miss M. Pawlik — 7-6, 6-3
- Miss W. M. Turnbull — 6-4, 6-1
- Mrs. H. W. Wiesner — 7-6, 6-4
- Miss S. Amiach — 6-4, 5-7, 6-4
- Miss R. Reggi — 6-4, 6-0
- Miss J. Halard — 7-5, 7-5
- Miss A. Sanchez Vicario ⑦ — 6-2, 7-5
- Mrs. C. M. Evert ④ — 6-1, 6-1
- Miss Hu Na
- Miss A. E. Hobbs — 6-7, 6-4, 6-4
- Miss G. Miro — 6-1, 6-3
- Miss C. J. Wood — 6-0, 6-2
- Miss P. A. Fendick — 6-3, 7-5
- Miss A. Devries — 6-7, 6-4, 6-4
- Miss S. Stafford — 7-6, 7-5
- Miss J. Novotna ⑩ — 6-2, 6-1
- Miss E. M. Burgin — 6-4, 3-6, 6-2
- Miss C. E. Cunningham — 6-4, 6-4
- Miss K. M. Adams — 7-5, 6-3
- Miss L. Golarsa
- Miss M. Strandlund — 6-4, 3-6, 6-3
- Miss L. Field — 6-4, 3-6, 8-6
- Miss Z. L. Garrison ⑤ — 6-1, 6-2
- Miss H. Sukova ⑥ — 6-4, 6-4
- Miss D. S. Van Rensburg — 6-3, 6-1
- Miss A. B. Henricksson — 6-3, 7-6
- Miss C. Kohde-Kilsch — 6-4, 6-2
- Miss I. Demongeot — 6-1, 6-3
- Miss C. Lindqvist — 6-4, 6-2
- Miss E. S. Pfaff — 6-4, 6-3
- Miss N. Zvereva ⑨ — 6-7, 6-2, 6-0
- Miss M. J. Fernandez ⑫ — 6-4, 7-5
- Miss L. K. Allen — 7-6, 6-2
- Miss C. Tanvier — 6-2, 6-3
- Miss A. Frazier — 6-2, 6-4
- Miss T. Scheuer-Larsen — 6-1, 6-1
- Mrs. P. D. Smylie — 6-4, 6-0
- Miss R. D. Fairbank — 6-4, 6-3
- Miss G. Sabatini ③ — 6-1, 6-0
- Miss P. H. Shriver ⑧ — 6-2, 6-1
- Miss S. L. Gomer — 6-3, 6-2
- Miss V. Lake — 7-6, 3-6, 6-1
- Mrs. S. W. Magers — 7-6, 6-4
- Miss I. Budarova — 6-4, 3-6, 6-2
- Miss J.-A. Faull — 4-6, 6-2, 8-6
- Mrs. L. Gildemeister — 6-4, 6-2
- Miss S. P. Sloane ⑯ — 6-4, 6-0
- Miss H. Mandlikova ⑭ — 7-5, 6-3
- Miss C. Suire — 7-5, 5-7, 6-1
- Miss D. L. Faber — 6-1, 2-6, 6-2
- Miss J. G. Thompson — 6-1, 4-6, 8-6
- Miss N. Provis — 7-6, 7-6
- Miss R. M. White — 7-5, 1-6, 6-2
- Miss K. Radford — 6-3, 7-6
- Miss M. Navratilova ② — 6-3, 6-2

THIRD ROUND

- Miss S. Graf ① — 6-2, 6-1
- Miss A. L. Minter — 6-2, 6-0
- Miss E. Sviglerova — 7-6, 7-5
- Miss M. Seles ⑪ — 6-2, 6-4
- Miss L. M. McNeil ⑮ — 6-1, 6-3
- Mrs. H. W. Wiesner — 6-4, 7-5
- Miss R. Reggi — 7-6, 6-4
- Miss A. Sanchez Vicario ⑦ — 6-4, 6-3
- Mrs. C. M. Evert ④ — 7-5, 6-3
- Miss A. E. Hobbs — 5-7, 6-2, 6-4
- Miss P. A. Fendick — 6-1, 6-4
- Miss S. Stafford — 7-6, 7-5
- Miss J. Novotna ⑩ — 6-4, 3-6, 6-2
- Miss K. M. Adams — 6-1, 6-2
- Miss L. Golarsa — 6-4, 4-6, 6-1
- Miss L. Field — 1-6, 6-2, 7-5
- Miss H. Sukova ⑥ — 6-3, 6-3
- Miss C. Kohde-Kilsch — 6-4, 6-1
- Miss C. Lindqvist — 6-3, 6-1
- Miss N. Zvereva ⑨ — 6-2, 6-3
- Miss M. J. Fernandez ⑫ — 6-4, 6-1
- Miss C. Tanvier — 6-3, 6-1
- Mrs. P. D. Smylie — 6-1, 7-6, 6-1
- Miss R. D. Fairbank — 6-4, 6-3
- Miss P. H. Shriver ⑧ — 6-4, 3-6, 8-6
- Mrs. S. W. Magers — 6-2, 6-3
- Miss J.-A. Faull — 6-3, 6-0
- Mrs. L. Gildemeister — 6-3, 7-5
- Miss H. Mandlikova ⑭ — 6-1, 6-3
- Miss D. L. Faber — 7-6, 4-1 Rtd
- Miss N. Provis — 3-6, 6-3, 6-3
- Miss M. Navratilova ② — 3-6, 6-3, 6-3

FOURTH ROUND

- Miss S. Graf ① — 6-2, 6-0
- Miss M. Seles ⑪ — 6-4, 6-3
- Miss L. M. McNeil ⑮ — 5-7, 6-2, 6-4
- Miss A. Sanchez Vicario ⑦ — 4-6, 6-3, 7-5
- Mrs. C. M. Evert ④ — 6-4, 6-1
- Miss P. A. Fendick — 2-6, 6-1, 6-3
- Miss J. Novotna ⑩ — 6-4, 6-1
- Miss L. Golarsa — 6-4, 7-6
- Miss H. Sukova ⑥ — 4-6, 6-3, 6-3
- Miss C. Lindqvist — 7-6, 4-6, 6-4
- Miss M. J. Fernandez ⑫ — 4-6, 6-2, 6-4
- Miss R. D. Fairbank — 6-3, 6-3
- Mrs. S. W. Magers — 2-6, 6-2, 12-10
- Miss J.-A. Faull — 6-3, 7-6
- Miss H. Mandlikova ⑭ — 6-2, 6-4
- Miss M. Navratilova ② — 6-0, 6-3

QUARTER-FINALS

- Miss S. Graf ① — 6-1, 6-3
- Miss A. Sanchez Vicario ⑦ — 6-3, 2-6, 6-1
- Mrs. C. M. Evert ④ — 6-2, 6-2
- Miss L. Golarsa — 7-6 (7-4), 2-6, 6-4
- Miss C. Lindqvist — 6-4, 7-6 (7-5)
- Miss R. D. Fairbank — 6-4, 2-6, 6-0
- Mrs. S. W. Magers — 6-7 (5-7), 6-1, 6-0
- Miss M. Navratilova ② — 6-3, 6-2

SEMI-FINALS

- Miss S. Graf ① — 7-5, 6-1
- Mrs. C. M. Evert ④ — 6-3, 2-6, 7-5
- Miss C. Lindqvist — 7-5, 5-7
- Miss M. Navratilova ② — 6-1, 6-2

FINAL

- Miss S. Graf ① — 6-2, 6-1
- Miss M. Navratilova ② — 7-6 (7-5), 6-2

CHAMPION

Miss S. Graf ① — 6-2, 6-7 (1-7), 6-1

Heavy type denotes seeded players. The encircled figure against names denotes the order in which they have been seeded. (W) = Wild card. (Q) = Qualifier. (L) = Lucky loser. The Matches will be the best of three sets.

EVENT IV.—THE LADIES' DOUBLES CHAMPIONSHIP

Holders: Miss S. GRAF and Miss G. SABATINI

The Winners will become the holders, for the year, of the CHALLENGE CUP presented by H.R.H. PRINCESS MARINA, DUCHESS OF KENT, the late President of The All England Lawn Tennis and Croquet Club. The Winners will receive silver replicas of the Challenge Cup. A personal prize and a Silver Medal will be presented to each of the Runners-up and a Bronze Medal to each defeated Semi-finalist.

FIRST ROUND

1	**Miss M. Navratilova and Miss P. H. Shriver ①**
2	Miss I. Budarova and Miss R. Rajchrtova
3	Miss T. Phelps and Miss R. Reggi
(Q) 4	Miss R. Hiraki and Miss A. Van Buuren
(Q) 5	Miss P. Hy and Miss M. McGrath
6	Miss E. A. Herr and Miss C. S. Reynolds
(W) 7	Miss S. L. Gomer and Miss J. A. Salmon
8	**Miss E. M. Burgin and Miss R. D. Fairbank ⑨**
9	**Miss B. Schultz and Miss A. Temesvari ⑭**
10	Miss L. Golarsa and Miss S. Goles
11	Miss L. Field and Miss H. D. Witvoet
(L) 12	Miss A. M. Fernandez and Miss T. Zambrzycki
13	Miss S. Amiach and Miss M. Strandlund
14	Miss A. L. Minter and Miss J. A. Richardson
15	Miss C. MacGregor and Miss C. B. MacGregor
16	**Mrs. P. D. Smylie and Miss W. M. Turnbull ⑧**
17	**Miss J. Novotna and Miss H. Sukova ③**
(W) 18	Miss A. L. Grunfeld and Miss J. Louis
19	Miss C. Bakkum and Miss N. A. M. Jagerman
20	Miss B. Bunge and Miss C. Lindqvist
(Q) 21	Miss M. Kidowaki and Miss A. Nishiya
22	Miss B. C. Potter and Miss K. S. Rinaldi
23	Miss S. L. Collins and Miss E. Hakami
24	**Miss M. M. Bollegraf and Miss E. S. Pfaff ⑫**
25	**Mrs. C. M. Evert and Miss H. Mandlikova ⑯**
26	Miss C. Benjamin and Miss J. C. Kaplan
27	Miss L. K. Allen and Miss M. Van Nostrand
28	Miss A. Dechaume and Miss E. Derly
29	Miss L. Barnard and Miss K. T. Schimper
30	Mrs. P. F. Daniels and Miss A. B. Henricksson
31	Miss A. Sanchez Vicario and Mrs. H. W. Wiesner
32	**Miss G. Fernandez and Miss L. M. McNeil ⑥**
33	**Miss S. Graf and Miss G. Sabatini ⑤**
(W) 34	Miss J. Holden and Miss C. Pollard
35	Miss L. J. Gregory and Mrs. S. W. Magers
36	Miss J.-A. Faull and Miss H. Kelesi
37	Miss M. Grossi and Miss B. Romano
38	Miss H. Sprung and Miss K. A. Steinmetz
39	Miss N. Herreman and Miss M. Paz
40	**Miss J. M. Byrne and Miss R. M. White ⑬**
41	**Miss I. Demongeot and Miss N. Tauziat ⑩**
42	Miss Hu Na and Miss S. Stafford
43	Miss L. Antonoplis and Miss A. Scott
44	Miss N. Provis and Miss E. Reinach
45	Miss I. Driehuis and Miss A. Frazier
(W) 46	Miss B. A. Borneo and Miss C. J. Wood
47	Miss I. Kuczynska and Miss J. Pospisilova
48	**Miss P. A. Fendick and Miss J. M. Hetherington④**
49	**Miss K. M. Adams and Miss Z. L. Garrison⑦**
(Q) 50	Miss K. McDonald and Miss K. Radford
51	Miss J. Fuchs and Miss S. Smoller
52	Miss R. Casals and Mrs. M. H. Pete
53	Miss C. Kohde-Kilsch and Miss C. Porwik
54	Miss M. Lindstrom and Miss H. A. Ludloff
55	Miss M. C. Norwood and Miss J. E. Thomas
(L) 56	Miss L. A. Eldredge and Miss L. O'Halloran
57	**Miss T. Scheuer-Larsen and Miss C. Tanvier⑮**
58	Miss P. Barg and Miss R. Reis
59	Miss B. Nagelsen and Miss D. S. Van Rensburg
60	Mrs. T. A. Harper and Miss W. E. White
61	Miss N. Miyagi and Miss T. J. Morton
62	Miss M. Jaggard and Miss L. O'Neill
63	Miss A. E. Hobbs and Miss C. Suire
64	**Miss L. Savchenko and Miss N. Zvereva ②**

SECOND ROUND

Miss M. Navratilova and Miss P. H. Shriver ①	6-0, 6-0
Miss T. Phelps and Miss R. Reggi	6-4, 7-5
Miss E. A. Herr and Miss C. S. Reynolds	0-6, 6-1, 6-4
Miss E. M. Burgin and Miss R. D. Fairbank ⑨	7-6, 6-4
Miss B. Schultz and Miss A. Temesvari ⑭	6-3, 6-3
Miss L. Field and Miss H. D. Witvoet	6-1, 6-3
Miss A. L. Minter and Miss J. A. Richardson	6-4, 3-6, 7-5
Mrs. P. D. Smylie and Miss W. M. Turnbull ⑧	6-7, 6-4, 6-2
Miss J. Novotna and Miss H. Sukova ③	6-1, 6-0
Miss B. Bunge and Miss C. Lindqvist	4-6, 7-6, 6-4
Miss B. C. Potter and Miss K. S. Rinaldi	5-7, 6-1, 6-2
Miss M. M. Bollegraf and Miss E. S. Pfaff ⑫	7-6, 6-2
Mrs. C. M. Evert and Miss H. Mandlikova ⑯	6-1, 6-2
Miss L. K. Allen and Miss M. Van Nostrand	6-4, 6-3
Miss L. Barnard and Miss K. T. Schimper	7-6, 6-4
Miss G. Fernandez and Miss L. M. McNeil ⑥	6-2, 6-2
Miss S. Graf and Miss G. Sabatini ⑤	6-2, 6-2
Miss L. J. Gregory and Mrs. S. W. Magers	6-1, 6-2
Miss H. Sprung and Miss K. A. Steinmetz	1-6, 6-4, 6-2
Miss J. M. Byrne and Miss R. M. White ⑬	6-4, 6-1
Miss Hu Na and Miss S. Stafford	6-3, 2-6, 9-7
Miss N. Provis and Miss E. Reinach	3-6, 6-4, 7-5
Miss P. A. Fendick and Miss J. M. Hetherington④	6-3, 6-4
Miss K. M. Adams and Miss Z. L. Garrison ⑦	6-4, 6-2
Miss R. Casals and Mrs. M. H. Pete	6-4, 6-2
Miss C. Kohde-Kilsch and Miss C. Porwik	6-4, 6-4
Miss L. A. Eldredge and Miss L. O'Halloran	1-6, 6-4, 6-2
Miss P. Barg and Miss R. Reis	1-6, 6-1, 6-4
Mrs. T. A. Harper and Miss W. E. White	6-2, 6-4
Miss M. Jaggard and Miss L. O'Neill	2-6, 6-3, 6-3
Miss L. Savchenko and Miss N. Zvereva ②	6-1, 6-3

THIRD ROUND

Miss M. Navratilova and Miss P. H. Shriver ①	6-0, 6-3
Miss E. M. Burgin and Miss R. D. Fairbank ⑨	6-1, 7-5
Miss B. Schultz and Miss A. Temesvari ⑭	6-3, 7-5
Mrs. P. D. Smylie and Miss W. M. Turnbull ⑧	4-6, 6-3, 6-3
Miss J. Novotna and Miss H. Sukova ③	7-6, 7-5
Miss M. M. Bollegraf and Miss E. S. Pfaff ⑫	7-6, 2-2 Ret'd
Mrs. C. M. Evert and Miss H. Mandlikova ⑯	6-3, 6-3
Miss G. Fernandez and Miss L. M. McNeil ⑥	6-3, 6-2
Miss S. Graf and Miss G. Sabatini ⑤	6-3, 6-0
Miss J. M. Byrne and Miss R. M. White ⑬	6-4, 6-1
Miss N. Provis and Miss E. Reinach	6-1, 4-6, 6-3
Miss P. A. Fendick and Miss J. M. Hetherington④	6-0, 6-2
Miss K. M. Adams and Miss Z. L. Garrison ⑦	6-4, 6-3
Miss C. Kohde-Kilsch and Miss C. Porwik	6-1, 6-2
Mrs. T. A. Harper and Miss W. E. White	6-2, 3-6, 6-1
Miss L. Savchenko and Miss N. Zvereva ②	6-1, 7-5

QUARTER-FINALS

Miss M. Navratilova and Miss P. H. Shriver ①	6-4, 7-6 (7-4)
Miss B. Schultz and Miss A. Temesvari ⑭	6-1, 6-3
Miss J. Novotna and Miss H. Sukova ③	6-1, 6-1
Miss G. Fernandez and Miss L. M. McNeil ⑥	6-4, 6-4
Miss S. Graf and Miss G. Sabatini ⑤	6-2, 6-3
Miss N. Provis and Miss E. Reinach	7-5, 4-6, 6-3
Miss K. M. Adams and Miss Z. L. Garrison ⑦	6-7 (3-7), 6-3, 6-0
Miss L. Savchenko and Miss N. Zvereva ②	6-2, 6-1

SEMI-FINALS

Miss M. Navratilova and Miss P. H. Shriver ①	7-5, 6-7 (5-1), 7-5
Miss J. Novotna and Miss H. Sukova ③	1-6, 6-1, 6-4
Miss N. Provis and Miss E. Reinach	7-6 (7-0), 6-4
Miss L. Savchenko and Miss N. Zvereva ②	6-3, 7-6 (7-5)

FINAL

Miss J. Novotna and Miss H. Sukova ③	7-6 (7-4), 7-5
Miss L. Savchenko and Miss N. Zvereva ②	6-2, 6-2

Winners: Miss J. Novotna and Miss H. Sukova ③ 6-1, 6-2

Heavy type denotes seeded players. The encircled figure against names denotes the order in which they have been seeded. (W) = Wild card. (Q) = Qualifier. (L) = Lucky loser. The Matches will be the best of three sets.

EVENT V.—THE MIXED DOUBLES CHAMPIONSHIP

Holders: S. E. STEWART and Miss Z. L. GARRISON

The Winners will become the holders, for the year, of the CHALLENGE CUP presented by the family of the late Mr. S. H. SMITH. The Winners will receive silver replicas of the Challenge Cup. A personal prize and a Silver Medal will be presented to each of the Runners-up and a Bronze Medal to each defeated Semi-finalist.

FIRST ROUND

1. J. Pugh and Miss J. Novotna ①
2. R. Smith and Miss K. M. Adams
3. R. A. Reneberg and Mrs. T. A. Harper
4. (L) P. Palandjian and Miss J. E. Thomas
5. B. Willenborg and Miss P. Barg
6. (L) B. Talbot and Miss D. L. Faber
7. G. Layendecker and Miss L. Field
8. **M. Mortensen and Miss T. Scheuer-Larsen ⑯**
9. **T. Nijssen and Miss M. M. Bollegraf ⑫**
10. G. Van Emburgh and Miss J. Smoller
11. (W) N. A. Fulwood and Miss J. A. Salmon
12. (Q) S. Furlong and Miss K. Radford
13. (L) P. Wright and Miss J. Pospisilova
14. D. Wheaton and Miss M. J. Fernandez
15. (L) C. Honey and Miss A. Van Buuren
16. **M. Woodforde and Miss H. Mandlikova ⑧**
17. **R. Seguso and Miss L. M. McNeil ④**
18. E. Edwards and Miss M. Van Nostrand
19. (Q) C. Banducci and Miss H. A. Ludloff
20. S. Devries and Miss R. Casals
21. L. Warder and Miss B. A. Borneo
22. A. N. Castle and Miss A. E. Hobbs
23. J. Letts and Miss C. B. MacGregor
24. **D. T. Visser and Miss R. D. Fairbank ⑨**
25. **J. Lozano and Miss C. Suire ⑬**
26. G. Michibata and Miss M. C. Norwood
27. B. Dyke and Miss M. Jaggard
28. B. Man Son Hing and Miss C. MacGregor
29. R. Deppe and Miss D. S. Van Rensburg
30. (W) J. M. Goodall and Miss V. Lake
31. C. Suk and Miss I. Budarova
32. **J. B. Fitzgerald and Mrs. P. D. Smylie ⑤**
33. **P. McEnroe and Miss G. Fernandez ⑦**
34. J. Rive and Miss B. C. Potter
35. B. Pearce and Miss C. S. Reynolds
36. (L) L. Herrera and Miss C. Tessi
37. D. Cahill and Miss N. Provis
38. L. B. Jensen and Miss J. Fuchs
39. M. Schapers and Miss B. Schultz
40. **P. Aldrich and Miss E. Reinach ⑮**
41. **P. Doohan and Miss E. M. Burgin ⑩**
42. S. Youl and Miss A. L. Minter
43. S. M. Shaw and Miss C. Lindqvist
44. (L) N. Borwick and Miss P. Moreno
45. (W) J. M. Lloyd and Miss W. M. Turnbull
46. T. Siegel and Miss J. C. Kaplan
47. (L) L. Scott and Miss T. Zambrzycki
48. **R. Leach and Miss B. Nagelsen ③**
49. (W) **S. E. Stewart and Miss Z. L. Garrison ⑥**
50. R. Vogel and Miss J. Pospisilova
51. T. Woodbridge and Miss W. E. White
52. (L) G. Pfitzner and Miss H. Sprung
53. (Q) B. H. Levine and Miss M. McGrath
54. K. Jones and Mrs. S. W. Magers
55. G. Connell and Miss P. Hy
56. **M. Kratzmann and Miss J. M. Byrne ⑭**
57. **R. W. Van't Hof and Miss R. M. White ⑪**
58. T. Svantesson and Miss L. O'Neill
59. J. Stoltenberg and Miss J.-A. Faull
60. J. Fleurian and Miss S. L. Collins
61. N. Broad and Miss T. Phelps
62. (W) D. C. Felgate and Miss C. J. Wood
63. T. Pawsat and Miss E. A. Herr
64. **K. Flach and Miss J. M. Hetherington ②**

SECOND ROUND

- J. Pugh and Miss J. Novotna ① 6–4, 6–4
- R. A. Reneberg and Mrs. T. A. Harper 6–1, 6–2
- B. Talbot and Miss D. L. Faber 7–6, 6–4
- **M. Mortensen and Miss T. Scheuer-Larsen ⑯** 5–7, 6–4, 6–4
- T. Nijssen and Miss M. M. Bollegraf ⑫ 6–3, 6–4
- S. Furlong and Miss K. Radford 2–6, 6–4, 6–3
- D. Wheaton and Miss M. J. Fernandez 6–4, 7–6
- **M. Woodforde and Miss H. Mandlikova ⑧** 6–4, 6–2
- R. Seguso and Miss L. M. McNeil ④ 6–2, 6–4
- C. Banducci and Miss H. A. Ludloff 6–4, 7–6
- A. N. Castle and Miss A. E. Hobbs 6–3, 5–7, 6–4
- **D. T. Visser and Miss R. D. Fairbank ⑨** 6–2, 6–3
- J. Lozano and Miss C. Suire ⑬ 6–3, 6–2
- B. Dyke and Miss M. Jaggard 6–0, 6–3
- R. Deppe and Miss D. S. Van Rensburg 6–3, 7–5
- **J. B. Fitzgerald and Mrs. P. D. Smylie ⑤** 6–4, 6–4
- P. McEnroe and Miss G. Fernandez ⑦ 7–6, 6–1
- B. Pearce and Miss C. S. Reynolds 7–5, 6–1
- D. Cahill and Miss N. Provis 6–2, 6–0
- M. Schapers and Miss B. Schultz 6–4, 1–6, 6–3
- **P. Doohan and Miss E. M. Burgin ⑩** 6–1, 3–6, 6–3
- N. Borwick and Miss P. Moreno 4–6, 7–5, 8–6
- J. M. Lloyd and Miss W. M. Turnbull 6–3, 6–7, 6–4
- **R. Leach and Miss B. Nagelsen ③** 6–3, 3–6, 6–3
- S. E. Stewart and Miss Z. L. Garrison ⑥ 6–4, 6–4
- T. Woodbridge and Miss W. E. White 6–2, 6–1
- K. Jones and Mrs. S. W. Magers 7–6, 6–2
- **M. Kratzmann and Miss J. M. Byrne ⑭** 6–7, 6–4, 6–2
- R. W. Van't Hof and Miss R. M. White ⑪ 6–1, 6–3
- J. Stoltenberg and Miss J.-A. Faull 7–6, 6–3
- N. Broad and Miss T. Phelps 6–1, 6–2
- T. Pawsat and Miss E. A. Herr 7–6, 6–4

THIRD ROUND

- **J. Pugh and Miss J. Novotna ①** 6–3, 6–2
- M. Mortensen and Miss T. Scheuer-Larsen ⑯ 6–3, 6–3
- T. Nijssen and Miss M. M. Bollegraf ⑫ 7–5, 6–4
- D. Wheaton and Miss M. J. Fernandez 7–6, 3–6, 6–4
- **R. Seguso and Miss L. M. McNeil ④** 6–4, 6–1
- **D. T. Visser and Miss R. D. Fairbank ⑨** 6–4, 7–6
- B. Dyke and Miss M. Jaggard 1–6, 6–3, 6–2
- R. Deppe and Miss D. S. Van Rensburg 5–7, 6–4, 11–9
- **P. McEnroe and Miss G. Fernandez ⑦** 7–6, 7–6
- D. Cahill and Miss N. Provis 5–7, 6–2, 6–3
- **P. Doohan and Miss E. M. Burgin ⑩** 6–2, 6–3
- R. Leach and Miss B. Nagelsen ③ w/o
- S. E. Stewart and Miss Z. L. Garrison ⑥ 6–4, 6–4
- **M. Kratzmann and Miss J. M. Byrne ⑭** 6–1, 6–4
- J. Stoltenberg and Miss J.-A. Faull 6–3, 3–6, 6–3
- N. Broad and Miss T. Phelps 3–6, 7–6, 6–2

QUARTER-FINALS

- **J. Pugh and Miss J. Novotna ①** 6–2, 7–5
- D. Wheaton and Miss M. J. Fernandez 6–2, 2–6, 6–2
- **R. Seguso and Miss L. M. McNeil ④** 3–6, 7–5, 6–2
- R. Deppe and Miss D. S. Van Rensburg 7–5, 7–6 (10–8)
- D. Cahill and Miss N. Provis 6–2, 4–6, 6–4
- **R. Leach and Miss B. Nagelsen ③** 6–4, 5–7, 6–4
- **M. Kratzmann and Miss J. M. Byrne ⑭** 6–2, 6–4
- N. Broad and Miss T. Phelps 7–6 (7–2), 6–4

SEMI-FINALS

- **J. Pugh and Miss J. Novotna ①** 6–4, 9–7
- **R. Seguso and Miss L. M. McNeil ④** 2–6, 6–4, 6–4
- **R. Leach and Miss B. Nagelsen ③** w/o
- M. Kratzmann and Miss J. M. Byrne ⑭ 3–6, 7–5, 13–11

FINAL

- **J. Pugh and Miss J. Novotna ①** 6–1, 5–7, 6–4
- M. Kratzmann and Miss J. M. Byrne ⑭ 6–4, 7–6, (7–2)

WINNER

J. Pugh and Miss J. Novotna ① 6–4, 5–7, 6–4

Heavy type denotes seeded players. The encircled figure against names denotes the order in which they have been seeded. (W) = Wild card. (Q) = Qualifier. (L) = Lucky loser. The Matches will be the best of three sets.

EVENT VI.—THE ALL ENGLAND LADIES' PLATE

Holder: Mrs. S. W. MAGERS

Players who are beaten in the first or second round of the Ladies' Singles Championship and also players only taking part in the Doubles events are entitled to enter for this Event. The Winner will become the holder, for the year only, of a Silver Cup "The All England Ladies' Plate", presented to The All England Lawn Tennis and Croquet Club by the late Mr. A. H. RISELEY, O.B.E. The Winner will receive a silver miniature of the Trophy.

FIRST ROUND

1	**Miss T. Phelps** ①	(USA)
2	Bye	
3	Miss T. Zambrzycki	(BRA)
4	Miss J. A. Richardson	(NZL)
5	Miss J. A. Salmon	(GBR)
6	Miss T. J. Morton	(AUS)
7	Bye	
8	**Miss W. E. White** ⑫	(USA)
9	**Mrs. T. A. Harper** ⑬	(USA)
10	Bye	
11	Miss V. Lake	(GBR)
12	Miss Hu Na	(USA)
13	Miss P. Barg	(USA)
14	Miss R. Reis	(USA)
15	Bye	
16	**Miss G. Fernandez** ⑥	(USA)
17	**Miss R. M. White** ④	(USA)
18	Bye	
19	Miss P. Hy	(HKG)
20	Miss B. A. Borneo	(GBR)
21	Miss J. Smoller	(USA)
22	Miss M. Jaggard	(AUS)
23	Bye	
24	**Miss M. Van Nostrand** ⑯	(USA)
25	**Miss S. L. Gomer** ⑨	(GBR)
26	Bye	
27	Miss A. L. Grunfeld	(GBR)
28	Miss D. A. Graham	(USA)
29	Miss L. Barnard	(ZAF)
30	Miss M. Javer	(GBR)
31	Bye	
32	**Miss A. Temesvari** ⑦	(HUN)
33	Miss J. C. Kaplan	(USA)
34	Bye	
35	Miss C. Suire	(FRA)
36	Miss K. Kessaris	(USA)
37	Miss S. Amiach	(FRA)
38	Miss A. Simpkin	(GBR)
39	Bye	
40	**Miss C. E. Cunningham** ⑪	(USA)
41	**Miss M. Paz** ⑩	(ARG)
42	Bye	
43	Miss J. Louis	(GBR)
44	Miss I. Kuczynska	(POL)
45	Miss L. Antonoplis	(USA)
46	Miss L. O'Neill	(AUS)
47	Bye	
48	**Miss J. M. Byrne** ③	(AUS)
49	**Miss E. Reinach** ⑤	(ZAF)
50	Bye	
51	Miss A. Scott	(AUS)
52	Miss J. E. Thomas	(USA)
53	Miss S. L. Collins	(USA)
54	Miss I. Budarova	(CSK)
55	Bye	
56	**Miss C. MacGregor** ⑮	(USA)
57	**Miss C. Benjamin** ⑭	(USA)
58	Bye	
59	Miss C. J. Wood	(GBR)
60	Miss H. D. Witvoet	(NLD)
61	Miss K. T. Schimper	(ZAF)
62	Miss M. McGrath	(USA)
63	Bye	
64	**Miss A. Frazier** ②	(USA)

SECOND ROUND

- Miss T. Phelps ①
- Miss T. Zambrzycki — 6–3, 7–6
- Miss T. J. Morton — 6–4, 3–6, 6–4
- Miss W. E. White ⑫
- Mrs. T. A. Harper ⑬
- Miss Hu Na — 6–3, 6–1
- Miss R. Reis — 6–3, 6–2
- Miss G. Fernandez ⑥
- Miss R. M. White ④
- Miss P. Hy — 7–6, 6–3
- Miss M. Jaggard — 5–3 Ret'd
- Miss M. Van Nostrand ⑯
- Miss S. L. Gomer ⑨
- Miss D. A. Graham — 6–1, 6–2
- Miss L. Barnard — 6–4, 7–6
- Miss A. Temesvari ⑦
- Miss J. C. Kaplan
- Miss C. Suire — 7–5, 7–6
- Miss S. Amiach — 6–3, 4–6, 6–4
- Miss C. E. Cunningham ⑪
- Miss M. Paz ⑩
- Miss I. Kuczynska — 1–6, 6–4, 6–4
- Miss L. Antonoplis — 6–2, 6–7, 6–4
- Miss J. M. Byrne ③
- Miss E. Reinach ⑤
- Miss A. Scott — 6–1, 6–4
- Miss S. L. Collins — 6–4, 6–3
- Miss C. MacGregor ⑮
- Miss C. Benjamin ⑭
- Miss C. J. Wood — 6–2, 6–2
- Miss M. McGrath — 7–5, 6–2
- Miss A. Frazier ②

THIRD ROUND

- Miss T. Phelps ① — 6–2, 6–3
- Miss W. E. White ⑫ — 6–4, 6–1
- Mrs. T. A. Harper ③ — 6–4, 6–1
- Miss G. Fernandez ⑥ — w/o
- Miss P. Hy — 4–6, 7–6, 9–7
- Miss M. Jaggard — 6–0, 7–6
- Miss S. L. Gomer ⑨ — 6–1, 6–4
- Miss A. Temesvari ⑦ — 6–4, 6–2
- Miss C. Suire — 6–2, 5–2 Ret'd
- Miss C. E. Cunningham ⑪ — w/o
- Miss I. Kuczynska — 6–2, 6–3
- Miss J. M. Byrne ③ — 6–7, 6–4, 6–0
- Miss E. Reinach ⑤ — 6–1, 6–4
- Miss C. MacGregor ⑮ — 6–3, 6–2
- Miss C. Benjamin ⑭ — 7–6, 7–5
- Miss A. Frazier ② — 7–5, 6–4

QUARTER-FINALS

- Miss W. E. White ⑫ — 6–1, 6–0
- Miss G. Fernandez ⑥ — 6–2, 6–1
- Miss M. Jaggard — 6–4, 1–0, Ret'd
- Miss S. L. Gomer ⑨ — 4–6, 6–3, 6–2
- Miss C. Suire — 6–0, 6–1
- Miss J. M. Byrne ③ — 6–4, 6–4
- Miss E. Reinach ⑤ — 6–0, 6–2
- Miss A. Frazier ② — 6–3, 6–2

SEMI-FINALS

- Miss W. E. White ⑫ — w/o
- Miss S. L. Gomer ⑨ — 6–4, 6–4
- Miss C. Suire — 6–3, 6–4
- Miss E. Reinach ⑤ — 6–3, 6–4

FINAL

- Miss W. E. White ⑫ — 7–6 (9–7), 6–1
- Miss E. Reinach ⑤ — 6–0, 6–4

WINNER

Miss W. E. White ⑫ — 6–3, 6–4

Heavy type denotes seeded players. The encircled figure against names denotes the order in which they have been seeded. The Matches will be the best of three sets.

EVENT VII.—THE 35 AND OVER GENTLEMEN'S INVITATION SINGLES   Holder: T. R. GULLIKSON

The Winner will become the holder, for the year only, of a Cup presented by The All England Lawn Tennis and Croquet Club. The Winner will receive a miniature Silver Salver, the Runner-up will be presented with a Silver Medal.

FIRST ROUND	QUARTER-FINALS	SEMI-FINALS	FINAL
1 **T. R. Gullikson** ① (USA) 2 R. W. Drysdale (GBR)	**T. R. Gullikson** ① 6–2, 6–2	**T. R. Gullikson** ① 7–6 (9–7), 6–4	
3 R. L. Stockton (USA) 4 J. G. Alexander (AUS)	R. L. Stockton 6–4, 6–2		T. R. Gullikson ① 6–4, 6–4
5 **M. R. Edmondson** ④ (AUS) 6 I. Nastase (ROM)	**M. R. Edmondson** ④ 6–4, 6–3	**M. R. Edmondson** ④ 6–3, 6–3	
7 T. S. Okker (NLD) 8 R. C. Lutz (USA)	R. C. Lutz 7–6 (7–2), 7–6 (7–5)		
9 A. A. Mayer (USA) 10 R. Taylor (GBR)	A. A. Mayer 6–3, 6–2	M. C. Riessen 6–3, 3–6, 6–3	
11 M. C. Riessen (USA) 12 **A. D. Roche** ③ (AUS)	M. C. Riessen 7–6 (7–2), 6–7 (2–7), 6–1		T. E. Gullikson ② 5–7, 6–4, 7–6 (7–5)
13 J. W. Feaver (GBR) 14 R. Tanner (USA)	R. Tanner 6–4, 7–5	T. E. Gullikson ② 6–2, 6–2	
15 J. Kodes (CSK) 16 **T. E. Gullikson** ② (USA)	**T. E. Gullikson** ② 6–2, 6–4		

Winner: T. R. Gullikson ① 7–5, 7–3

Heavy type denotes seeded players. The encircled figure against names denotes the order in which they have been seeded. (W) = Wild cards. The Matches will be the best of three sets.
The tie-break will operate at six games all in all three sets.

Event VIII.—THE 35 AND OVER GENTLEMEN'S INVITATION DOUBLES   Holders: R. A. J. HEWITT and F. D. McMILLAN

The Winners will become the holders, for the year only, of a Cup presented by The All England Lawn Tennis and Croquet Club. The Winners will receive miniature Silver Salvers, a Silver Medal will be presented to each of the Runners-up.

FIRST ROUND	SEMI-FINALS	FINAL
1 **R. A. J. Hewitt and F. D. McMillan** ① 2 R. C. Lutz and R. L. Stockton	R. C. Lutz and R. L. Stockton 6–3, 6–3	R. C. Lutz and R. L. Stockton 6–3, 6–4
3 **J. D. Newcombe and A. D. Roche** ④ 4 M. C. Riessen and S. E. Stewart	M. C. Riessen and S. E. Stewart 6–4, 6–2	
5 T. E. Gullikson and T. R. Gullikson 6 **R. L. Case and G. Masters** ③	T. E. Gullikson and T. R. Gullikson 6–1, 6–4	A. Amritraj and V. Amritraj 4–6, 6–3, 6–4
7 A. Amritraj and V. Amritraj 8 **K. R. Rosewall and F. S. Stolle** ②	A. Amritraj and V. Amritraj 6–2, 6–0	

Winners: A. Amritraj and V. Amritraj 6–3, 6–2

Heavy type denotes seeded players. The encircled figure against names denotes the order in which they have been seeded. (W) = Wild cards. The Matches will be the best of three sets.
The tie-break will operate at six games all in all two sets only.

151

The Winner will become the holder, for the year only, of a Cup presented by The All England Lawn Tennis and Croquet Club. The Winner and Runner-up will each receive a personal prize.

FIRST ROUND

1	**N. Kulti** ①	(SWE)
2	T. Tipene	(NZL)
3	B. Madsen	(HTI)
4	O. Kristiansson	(SWE)
5	B. Richardson	(AUS)
6	C. Paez	(CRI)
7	C. Marsh	(ZAF)
8	**D. Rikl** ⑮	(CSK)
9	**A. Thoms** ⑨	(DEU)
10	R. Ng	(HKG)
11	F. Bach	(NOR)
12	V. Frieden	(CHE)
13	D. R. Ireland	(GBR)
14	H. Tanizawa	(JPN)
15	M. Bayh	(DEU)
16	**F. Santoro** ⑧	(FRA)
17	**J. Anderson** ③	(AUS)
18	M. Achondo	(CHL)
19	P. Baumeler	(PER)
20	J. A. Haycock	(GBR)
21	J. M. Pohjola	(FIN)
22	T. Duangmanee	(THA)
23	M. Ruah	(VEN)
24	**M. Stringari** ⑬	(ARG)
25	**J. Stark** ⑪	(USA)
26	P. Alatorre	(MEX)
27	A. S. Hounsell	(ZWE)
28	S. Pospelov	(SUN)
29	J. J. Barton	(GBR)
30	I. Bozic	(YUG)
31	F. Dewulf	(BEL)
32	**W. Ferreira** ⑤	(ZAF)
33	**J. Palmer** ⑥	(USA)
34	M. Ondruska	(ZAF)
35	D. J. Draper	(GBR)
36	O. Fernandez	(MEX)
37	D. P. Harris	(GBR)
38	O. Bustos	(CHL)
39	C. H. Park	(KOR)
40	**M. S. Knowles** ⑫	(BHS)
41	**F. Meligeni** ⑭	(ARG)
42	M. Macaraeg	(PHI)
43	G. Lopez	(ESP)
44	B. Dabrowski	(POL)
45	E. Barbosa	(BRA)
46	J. Kodes	(CSK)
47	B. MacPhie	(USA)
48	**S. Pescosolido** ④	(ITA)
49	**J. Morgan** ⑦	(AUS)
50	R. Rajpal	(IND)
51	K. Masuda	(JPN)
52	P. Gainford	(GBR)
53	A. L. Foster	(GBR)
54	R. Alvarenga	(PRY)
55	T. Van Houdt	(BEL)
56	**L. E. Herrera** ⑩	(MEX)
57	**M. Damm** ⑯	(CSK)
58	J. Vila	(ESP)
59	T. El Sawy	(EGY)
60	Y. Yamamoto	(JPN)
61	L. Paes	(IND)
62	O. Weinberg	(ISR)
63	C. Engel	(BRA)
64	**T. Woodbridge** ②	(AUS)

SECOND ROUND

- N. Kulti ① — 6–4, 6–2
- O. Kristiansson — 6–3, 6–3
- B. Richardson — 6–0, 6–3
- D. Rikl ⑮ — 6–4, 7–6
- A. Thoms ⑨ — 6–4, 6–3
- V. Frieden — 7–6, 6–4
- D. R. Ireland — 7–5, 6–4
- F. Santoro ⑧ — 6–2, 7–6
- J. Anderson ③ — 6–3, 6–2
- J. A. Haycock — 6–2, 6–2
- T. Duangmanee — 6–4, 4–6, 7–5
- M. Ruah — 7–6, 6–3
- J. Stark ⑪ — 6–1, 6–4
- S. Pospelov — 6–2, 6–4
- J. J. Barton — 6–4, 5–7, 6–1
- W. Ferreira ⑤ — 6–3, 6–4
- J. Palmer ⑥ — 6–3, 3–6, 7–5
- O. Fernandez — 6–4, 6–1
- O. Bustos — 6–3, 3–6, 6–3
- M. S. Knowles ⑫ — 6–2, 7–5
- F. Meligeni ⑭
- G. Lopez — 7–6, 6–3
- J. Kodes — 3–6, 6–1, 6–3
- B. MacPhie — 7–5, 4–6, 6–2
- J. Morgan ⑦ — 6–3, 7–6
- K. Masuda — 6–2, 6–1
- A. L. Foster — 6–1, 6–2
- L. E. Herrera ⑩ — 6–0, 6–1
- M. Damm ⑯ — 2–6, 6–3, 6–2
- T. El Sawy — 7–6, 7–5
- O. Weinberg — 6–3, 7–6
- T. Woodbridge ② — 7–6, 6–2

THIRD ROUND

- N. Kulti ① — 7–6, 6–3
- B. Richardson — 6–4, 7–5
- A. Thoms ⑨ — 6–2, 6–4
- F. Santoro ⑧ — 6–4, 6–2
- J. Anderson ③ — 6–4, 6–3
- M. Ruah — 6–1, 6–0
- J. Stark ⑪ — 6–4, 6–2
- W. Ferreira ⑤ — 6–2, 6–3
- J. Palmer ⑥ — 4–6, 7–5, 8–6
- O. Bustos — 2–6, 6–3, 6–4
- G. Lopez — 7–5, 7–6
- B. MacPhie — 6–2, 6–1
- J. Morgan ⑦ — 7–5, 6–4
- L. E. Herrera ⑩ — 6–4, 6–2
- T. El Sawy — 6–2, 6–2
- T. Woodbridge ② — 6–2, 6–1

QUARTER-FINALS

- N. Kulti ① — 6–2, 6–4
- A. Thoms ⑨ — 6–3, 6–2
- J. Anderson ③ — 6–3, 7–6 (7–5)
- W. Ferreira ⑤ — 4–6, 7–6 (7–5), 6–3
- J. Palmer ⑥ — 6–3, 6–2
- B. MacPhie — 7–6 (7–2), 6–2
- L. E. Herrera ⑩ — 6–4, 6–2
- T. Woodbridge ② — 6–2, 6–3

SEMI-FINALS

- N. Kulti ① — 7–6 (7–1), 6–4
- W. Ferreira ⑤ — 6–2, 6–2
- B. MacPhie — 7–5, 3–6, 6–1
- T. Woodbridge ② — 6–1, 6–7 (4–7), 8–6

FINAL

- N. Kulti ① — 7–6 (7–4), 7–6 (7–2)
- T. Woodbridge ② — 4–6, 6–1, 8–6

Winner: N. Kulti ① — 6–4, 6–3

Heavy type denotes seeded players. The encircled figure against names denotes the order in which they have been seeded. The Committee reserves the right to alter the seeding order in the event of withdrawals. The Matches will be the best of three sets.

EVENT X.—THE BOYS' DOUBLES CHAMPIONSHIP   Holders: J. STOLTENBERG and T. WOODBRIDGE

The Winners and Runners-up will each receive a personal prize.

FIRST ROUND

1	**J. Anderson and T. Woodbridge** ①
2	O. Fernandez and M. Ruah
3	C. Marsh and M. Ondruska
4	P. Gainford and A. S. Hounsell
5	L. Paes and T. Tipene
6	F. Bach and J. M. Pohjola
7	D. Collins and S. Cornish
8	**J. Kodes and M. Stringari** ⑧
9	**J.-L. De Jager and W. Ferreira** ④
10	E. Barbosa and T. El Sawy
11	R. Holden and D. R. Ireland
12	M. Bayh and A. Thoms
13	B. Dabrowski and B. Madsen
14	A. L. Foster and J. A. Haycock
15	H. Tanizawa and Y. Yamamoto
16	**J. Morgan and B. Richardson** ⑤
17	**M. Damm and D. Rikl** ⑥
18	P. Baumeler and V. Frieden
19	T. Duangmanee and R. Ng
20	I. Bozic and S. Pospelov
21	J. J. Barton and D. J. Draper
22	C. Engel and F. Meligeni
23	A. Hunt and M. Zoricich
24	**O. Kristiansson and N. Kulti** ③
25	**P. Alatorre and M. S. Knowles** ⑦
26	B. MacPhie and R. Rajpal
27	K. Masuda and C. H. Park
28	M. Achondo and O. Bustos
29	D. P. Harris and J. Venison
30	F. Dewulf and T. Van Houdt
31	J. Vila and O. Weinberg
32	**J. Palmer and J. Stark** ②

SECOND ROUND

- J. Anderson and T. Woodbridge ① — 7–5, 6–4
- C. Marsh and M. Ondruska — 6–2, 7–5
- L. Paes and T. Tipene — 6–3, 6–2
- J. Kodes and M. Stringari ⑧ — 3–6, 7–6, 9–7
- J.-L. De Jager and W. Ferreira ④ — 6–1, 6–3
- M. Bayh and A. Thoms — 6–4, 6–3
- A. L. Foster and J. A. Haycock — 3–6, 7–6, 10–8
- J. Morgan and B. Richardson ⑤ — 6–3, 6–4
- M. Damm and D. Rikl ⑥ — 6–1, 7–6
- I. Bozic and S. Pospelov — 6–2, 6–3
- C. Engel and F. Meligeni — 6–7, 6–4, 10–8
- O. Kristiansson and N. Kulti ③ — 6–4, 6–4
- P. Alatorre and M. S. Knowles ⑦ — 7–6, 7–6
- M. Achondo and O. Bustos — 6–3, 7–5
- F. Dewulf and T. Van Houdt — 6–3, 3–6, 7–5
- J. Palmer and J. Stark ② — 7–6, 7–6

QUARTER-FINALS

- J. Anderson and T. Woodbridge ① — 6–2, 6–4
- L. Paes and T. Tipene — 4–6, 6–1, 7–5
- J.-L. De Jager and W. Ferreira ④ — 6–4, 4–6, 6–4
- J. Morgan and B. Richardson ⑤ — 6–4, 6–4
- M. Damm and D. Rikl ⑥ — 1–6, 6–1, 6–0
- O. Kristiansson and N. Kulti ③ — 6–2, 6–1
- P. Alatorre and M. S. Knowles ⑦ — 7–6 (7–5), 6–2
- J. Palmer and J. Stark ② — 6–2, 6–3

SEMI-FINALS

- J. Anderson and T. Woodbridge ① — 6–1, 7–5
- J.-L. De Jager and W. Ferreira ④ — 7–6 (7–4), 6–2
- M. Damm and D. Rikl ⑥ — 7–6 (9–7), 6–1
- J. Palmer and J. Stark ② — 6–1, 6–2

FINAL

- J.-L. De Jager and W. Ferreira ④ — 6–4, 5–7, 6–4
- J. Palmer and J. Stark ② — 6–3, 3–6, 6–4

Winners: J. Palmer and J. Stark ② — 7–6 (7–4), 7–6 (7–2)

Heavy type denotes seeded players. The encircled figure against names denotes the order in which they have been seeded. The Committee reserves the right to alter the seeding order in the event of withdrawals. The Matches will be the best of three sets.

The Winner will become the holder, for the year only, of a Cup presented by The All England Lawn Tennis and Croquet Club. The Winner and Runner-up will each receive a personal prize.

	FIRST ROUND	SECOND ROUND	THIRD ROUND	QUARTER-FINALS	SEMI-FINALS	FINAL
1	**Miss J.-A. Faull** ① (AUS)	**Miss J.-A. Faull** ① 6–0, 6–4				
2	Miss D. Gruber (CHE)		**Miss J.-A. Faull** ① 2–6, 7–5, 6–4			
3	Miss R. Walkerley (ZAF)	Miss K. A. Guse 6–1, 1–6, 6–0				
4	Miss K. A. Guse (AUS)			Miss N. Sawamatsu ⑥ 7–5, 7–6 (7–5)		
5	Miss O. Thampensri (THA)	Miss N. Van Lottum 6–2, 6–4				
6	Miss N. Van Lottum (FRA)		**Miss N. Sawamatsu** ⑥ 6–1, 6–2			
7	Miss S.-T. Wang (TAI)	**Miss N. Sawamatsu** ⑥ 6–3, 6–3				
8	**Miss N. Sawamatsu** ⑥ (JPN)				Miss N. Sawamatsu ⑥ 6–2, 6–1	
9	**Miss C. Tessi** ⑩ (ARG)	**Miss C. Tessi** ⑩ 6–1, 4–6, 6–4				
10	Miss S. Italiano (CAN)		**Miss C. Tessi** ⑩ 6–1, 3–6, 6–2			
11	Miss H. Hara (JPN)	Miss H. Hara 6–3, 6–7, 6–0				
12	Miss L. Barbour (ZWE)			Miss C. Tessi ⑩ 7–5, 4–6, 8–6		
13	Miss F. Khursheed (PAK)	Miss C. Rodriguez 6–3, 7–5				
14	Miss C. Rodriguez (PER)		**Miss E. Sviglerova** ⑦ 6–2, 6–1			
15	Miss M. Oldham (GBR)	**Miss E. Sviglerova** ⑦ 6–3, 6–4				
16	**Miss E. Sviglerova** ⑦ (CSK)					Miss A. Strnadova 6–2, 6–2
17	**Miss J. Capriati** ④ (USA)	**Miss J. Capriati** ④ 6–1, 6–1				
18	Miss J. Gunthrop (NZL)		**Miss J. Capriati** ④ 6–2, 6–2			
19	Miss B. Griffiths (GBR)	Miss K. Shibata 2–6, 6–2, 7–5				
20	Miss K. Shibata (JPN)			Miss J. Capriati ④ 6–1, 6–2		
21	Miss K. Sharpe (AUS)	Miss K. Sharpe 7–5, 6–7, 6–1				
22	Miss V. S. Humphreys-Davies (GBR)		Miss K. Sharpe 4–6, 6–3, 6–4			
23	Miss K. Teodorowicz (POL)	**Miss S. Testud** ⑭ 7–5, 2–6, 6–3				
24	**Miss S. Testud** ⑭ (FRA)				Miss A. Strnadova 6–2, 6–7 (3–7), 6–4	
25	**Miss S. L. Smith** ⑪ (GBR)	Miss R. Hiraki 6–3, 3–6, 6–3				
26	Miss R. Hiraki (JPN)		Miss A. Strnadova 6–2, 6–3			
27	Miss A. Strnadova (CSK)	Miss A. Strnadova 6–3, 6–2				
28	Miss S. Dubois (BEL)			Miss A. Strnadova 6–3, 6–1		
29	Miss M. Chmela (POL)	Miss M. Mraz 6–0, 6–1				
30	Miss M. Mraz (CAN)		Miss M. Mraz 6–2, 6–2			
31	Miss G. Devercelli (PER)	**Miss C. Caverzasio** ⑤ 6–2, 6–7, 6–3				
32	**Miss C. Caverzasio** ⑤ (ITA)					
33	**Miss M. McGrath** ⑥ (USA)	**Miss M. McGrath** ⑥ 6–1, 6–2				
34	Miss T. Gaddie (ZAF)		**Miss M. McGrath** ⑥ 6–3, 6–6, 6–3			
35	Miss R. Gaddie (ZAF)	Miss R. Gaddie 6–0, 6–1				
36	Miss N. Villarroel (BOL)			Miss M. McGrath ⑥ 7–5, 7–5		
37	Miss M. O. Kang (KOR)	Miss S. Ramon 6–2, 6–1				
38	Miss S. Ramon (ESP)		**Miss Y. Segal** ⑫ 6–7, 7–5, 6–2			
39	Miss C. Hall (GBR)	**Miss Y. Segal** ⑫ 6–0, 7–5				
40	**Miss Y. Segal** ⑫ (ISR)				Miss M. McGrath ⑥ 7–5, 6–3	
41	Miss M. T. Mair (GBR)	Miss E. Nieto 6–4, 6–3				
42	Miss E. Nieto (VEN)		Miss E. Nieto 6–2, 2–6, 6–2			
43	Miss P. Dechsupa (THA)	Miss A. Rohner 6–2, 6–3				
44	Miss A. Rohner (CHE)			Miss A. J. Coetzer ③ 6–3, 6–4		
45	Miss K. Godridge (AUS)	Miss K. Godridge 6–4, 6–1				
46	Miss B. Rittner (DEU)		**Miss A. J. Coetzer** ③ 6–3, 6–7, 6–4			
47	Miss L. Randmaa (CAN)	**Miss A. J. Coetzer** ③ 6–0, 6–0				
48	**Miss A. J. Coetzer** ③ (ZAF)					Miss M. McGrath ⑥ 7–6 (7–4), 6–1
49	**Miss K. Kessaris** ⑧ (USA)	**Miss K. Kessaris** ⑧ 6–2, 6–4				
50	Miss P. Cabezas (CHL)		**Miss K. Kessaris** ⑧ 6–3, 6–1			
51	Miss D. Aziz (BGD)	Miss S.-A. Siddall 6–0, 6–0				
52	Miss S.-A. Siddall (GBR)			Miss K. Kessaris ⑧ 6–0, 6–4		
53	Miss S. Castillejo (PHI)	Miss S. Bentley 6–1, 6–2				
54	Miss S. Bentley (GBR)		**Miss S. Farina** ⑨ 6–4, 6–2			
55	Miss S. Niland (IRE)	**Miss S. Farina** ⑨ 6–1, 7–5				
56	**Miss S. Farina** ⑨ (ITA)				Miss M. Anderson ⑮ 6–4, 7–5	
57	**Miss M. Anderson** ⑮ (ZAF)	**Miss M. Anderson** ⑮ 6–2, 6–1				
58	Miss S. Komleva (SUN)		Miss M. Anderson ⑮ 6–1, 6–4			
59	Miss N. Pratt (AUS)	Miss R. Viollet 6–2, 6–1				
60	Miss R. Viollet (GBR)			Miss M. Anderson ⑮ 6–4, 6–2		
61	Miss N. Biletskaia (SUN)	Miss A. Huber 6–3, 6–3				
62	Miss A. Huber (DEU)		**Miss C.E. Cunningham** ② 6–7, 7–5, 6–3			
63	Miss S. Reichel (AUT)	**Miss C. E. Cunningham** ② 6–0, 6–0				
64	**Miss C. E. Cunningham** ② (USA)					

Heavy type denotes seeded players. The encircled figure against names denotes the order in which they have been seeded. The Committee reserves the right to alter the seeding order in the event of withdrawals. The Matches will be the best of three sets.

EVENT XII.—THE GIRLS' DOUBLES CHAMPIONSHIP   Holders: Miss J. A. FAULL and Miss R. McQUILLAN

The Winners and Runners-up will each receive a personal prize.

	FIRST ROUND	SECOND ROUND	QUARTER-FINALS	SEMI-FINALS	FINAL
1	**Miss C. E. Cunningham and Miss K. Kessaris** ①		Miss R. Hiraki and Miss S.-T. Wang 7–6 (7–5), 6–0		
2	Miss R. Hiraki and Miss S.-T. Wang	Miss R. Hiraki and Miss S.-T. Wang 6–3, 6–1			
3	Miss H. E. Crook and Miss B. Griffiths			Miss R. Hiraki and Miss S.-T. Wang 7–5, 6–1	
4	Miss E. Nieto and Miss S. Ramon	Miss E. Nieto and Miss S. Ramon 7–5, 6–4			
5	Miss P. Cabezas and Miss P. Dechsupa		**Miss K. A. Guse and Miss N. Pratt** ⑦		
6	Miss S. Dubois and Miss K. Teodorowicz	Miss S. Dubois and Miss K. Teodorowicz 6–0, 6–2			
7	Miss S. Italiano and Miss M. Mraz				
8	**Miss K. A. Guse and Miss N. Pratt** ⑦	**Miss K. A. Guse and Miss N. Pratt** ⑦ 6–3, 6–4			
9	**Miss A. Strnadova and Miss E. Sviglerova** ③	**Miss A. Strnadova and Miss E. Sviglerova** ③		Miss A. Strnadova and Miss E. Sviglerova ③ 6–3, 7–5	
10	Miss N. Sawamatsu and Miss K. Shibata		Miss A. Strnadova and Miss E. Sviglerova ③ 3–6, 6–0, 6–2		
11	Miss S. Bentley and Miss M. T. Mair				
12	Miss G. Niland and Miss L. Randmaa	Miss G. Niland and Miss L. Randmaa 7–5, 3–6, 6–3			Miss A. Strnadova and Miss E. Sviglerova ③ 6–4, 4–6, 6–1
13	Miss R. Gaddie and Miss T. Gaddie		Miss M. Anderson and Miss A. J. Coetzer ⑥ 6–2, 6–0		
14	Miss M. Oldham and Miss S.-A. Siddall	Miss R. Gaddie and Miss T. Gaddie 6–2, 6–2			
15	Miss D. Gruber and Miss A. Rohner				
16	**Miss M. Anderson and Miss A. J. Coetzer** ⑥	**Miss M. Anderson and Miss A. J. Coetzer** ⑥ 6–2, 6–1			
17	**Miss C. Caverzasio and Miss S. Farina** ⑤		Miss C. Caverzasio and Miss S. Farina ⑤ 3–6, 6–3, 6–2		
18	Miss V.S. Humphreys-Davies and Miss R.F. Viollet	Miss C. Caverzasio and Miss S. Farina ⑤ 6–3, 6–1			
19	Miss L. Barbour and Miss R. Walkerley			Miss K. Godridge and Miss K. Sharpe ④ 4–6, 7–5, 7–5	
20	Miss A. L. Chorlton and Miss C. Rodriguez	Miss L. Barbour and Miss R. Walkerley 7–5, 6–0			
21	Miss S. Testud and Miss N. Van Lottum		**Miss K. Godridge and Miss K. Sharpe** ④ w/o		
22	Miss G. Devercelli and Miss N. Villarroel	Miss G. Devercelli and Miss N. Villarroel w/o			
23	Miss M. Chmela and Miss S. Reichel				Miss J. Capriati and Miss M. McGrath ② 6–4, 6–2
24	**Miss K. Godridge and Miss K. Sharpe** ④	**Miss K. Godridge and Miss K. Sharpe** ④ 6–4, 6–4			
25	**Miss S. L. Smith and Miss C. Tessi** ⑧	**Miss S. L. Smith and Miss C. Tessi** ⑧ 6–2, 6–1	Miss S. L. Smith and Miss C. Tessi ⑧ 6–2, 7–6 (7–3)		
26	Miss M. O. Kang and Miss O. Thampensri				
27	Miss S. Castillejo and Miss J. Gunthrop			Miss J. Capriati and Miss M. McGrath ② 6–2, 6–3	
28	Miss H. Hara and Miss F. Khursheed	Miss H. Hara and Miss F. Khursheed 3–6, 6–4, 6–3			
29	Miss N. Biletskaia and Miss S. Komleva		**Miss J. Capriati and Miss M. McGrath** ② 6–2, 5–7, 6–2		
30	Miss V. Graeme-Barber and Miss C. Hall	Miss N. Biletskaia and Miss S. Komleva 6–3, 3–6, 6–0			
31	Miss A. Huber and Miss M. B. Rittner				
32	**Miss J. Capriati and Miss M. McGrath** ②	**Miss J. Capriati and Miss M. McGrath** ② w/o			

Heavy type denotes seeded players. The encircled figure against names denotes the order in which they have been seeded. The Committee reserves the right to alter the seeding order in the event of withdrawals. The Matches will be the best of three sets.

THE CHAMPIONSHIP ROLL
Champions and Runners-up

MEN'S SINGLES

1877—S. W. Gore
 W. C. Marshall
1878—P. F. Hadow
 S. W. Gore
★1879—J. T. Hartley
 V. St. L. Goold
1880—J. T. Hartley
 H. F. Lawford
1881—W. Renshaw
 J. T. Hartley
1882—W. Renshaw
 E. Renshaw
1883—W. Renshaw
 E. Renshaw
1884—W. Renshaw
 H. F. Lawford
1885—W. Renshaw
 H. F. Lawford
1886—W. Renshaw
 H. F. Lawford
★1887—H. F. Lawford
 E. Renshaw
1888—E. Renshaw
 H. F. Lawford
1889—W. Renshaw
 E. Renshaw
1890—W. J. Hamilton
 W. Renshaw
★1891—W. Baddeley
 J. Pim
1892—W. Baddeley
 J. Pim
1893—J. Pim
 W. Baddeley
1894—J. Pim
 W. Baddeley
★1895—W. Baddeley
 W. V. Eaves

1896—H. S. Mahony
 W. Baddeley
1897—R. F. Doherty
 H. S. Mahony
1898—R. F. Doherty
 H. L. Doherty
1899—R. F. Doherty
 A. W. Gore
1900—R. F. Doherty
 S. H. Smith
1901—A. W. Gore
 R. F. Doherty
1902—H. L. Doherty
 A. W. Gore
1903—H. L. Doherty
 F. L. Riseley
1904—H. L. Doherty
 F. L. Riseley
1905—H. L. Doherty
 N. E. Brookes
1906—H. L. Doherty
 F. L. Riseley
★1907—N. E. Brookes
 A. W. Gore
★1908—A. W. Gore
 H. Roper Barrett
1909—A. W. Gore
 M. J. G. Ritchie
1910—A. F. Wilding
 A. W. Gore

1911—A. F. Wilding
 H. Roper Barrett
1912—A. F. Wilding
 A. W. Gore
1913—A. F. Wilding
 M. E. McLoughlin
1914—N. E. Brookes
 A. F. Wilding
1919—G. L. Patterson
 N. E. Brookes
1920—W. T. Tilden
 G. L. Patterson
1921—W. T. Tilden
 B. I. C. Norton
★†1922—G. L. Patterson
 R. Lycett
1923—W. M. Johnston
 F. T. Hunter
1924—J. Borotra
 R. Lacoste
1925—R. Lacoste
 J. Borotra
1926—J. Borotra
 H. Kinsey
1927—H. Cochet
 J. Borotra
1928—R. Lacoste
 H. Cochet
1929—H. Cochet
 J. Borotra

1930—W. T. Tilden
 W. Allison
1931—S. B. Wood
 F. X. Shields
1932—H. E. Vines
 H. W. Austin
1933—J. H. Crawford
 H. E. Vines
1934—F. J. Perry
 J. H. Crawford
1935—F. J. Perry
 G. von Cramm
1936—F. J. Perry
 G. von Cramm
★1937—J. D. Budge
 G. von Cramm
1938—J. D. Budge
 H. W. Austin
★1939—R. L. Riggs
 E. T. Cooke
★1946—Y. Petra
 G. E. Brown
1947—J. Kramer
 T. Brown
★1948—R. Falkenburg
 J. E. Bromwich
1949—F. R. Schroeder
 J. Drobny
★1950—B. Patty
 F. A. Sedgman
1951—R. Savitt
 K. McGregor
1952—F. A. Sedgman
 J. Drobny
★1953—V. Seixas
 K. Nielsen
1954—J. Drobny
 K. R. Rosewall

1955—T. Trabert
 K. Nielsen
★1956—L. A. Hoad
 K. R. Rosewall
1957—L. A. Hoad
 A. J. Cooper
★1958—A. J. Cooper
 N. A. Fraser
★1959—A. Olmedo
 R. Laver
★1960—N. A. Fraser
 R. Laver
1961—R. Laver
 C. R. McKinley
1962—R. Laver
 M. F. Mulligan
★1963—C. R. McKinley
 F. S. Stolle
1964—R. Emerson
 F. S. Stolle
1965—R. Emerson
 F. S. Stolle
1966—M. Santana
 R. D. Ralston
1967—J. D. Newcombe
 W. P. Bungert
1968—R. Laver
 A. D. Roche
1969—R. Laver
 J. D. Newcombe
1970—J. D. Newcombe
 K. R. Rosewall
1971—J. D. Newcombe
 S. R. Smith
★1972—S. R. Smith
 I. Nastase
★1973—J. Kodes
 A. Metreveli

1974—J. S. Connors
 K. R. Rosewall
1975—A. R. Ashe
 J. S. Connors
1976—B. Borg
 I. Nastase
1977—B. Borg
 J. S. Connors
1978—B. Borg
 J. S. Connors
1979—B. Borg
 R. Tanner
1980—B. Borg
 J. P. McEnroe
1981—J. P. McEnroe
 B. Borg
1982—J. S. Connors
 J. P. McEnroe
1983—J. P. McEnroe
 C. J. Lewis
1984—J. P. McEnroe
 J. S. Connors
1985—B. Becker
 K. Curren
1986—B. Becker
 I. Lendl
1987—P. Cash
 I. Lendl
1988—S. Edberg
 B. Becker
1989—B. Becker
 S. Edberg

MEN'S DOUBLES

1879—L. R. Erskine and H. F. Lawford
 F. Durant and G. E. Tabor
1880—W. Renshaw and E. Renshaw
 O. E. Woodhouse and C. J. Cole
1881—W. Renshaw and E. Renshaw
 W. J. Down and H. Vaughan
1882—J. T. Hartley and R. T. Richardson
 J. G. Horn and C. B. Russell
1883—C. W. Grinstead and C. E. Welldon
 C. B. Russell and R. T. Milford
1884—W. Renshaw and E. Renshaw
 E. W. Lewis and E. L. Williams
1885—W. Renshaw and E. Renshaw
 C. E. Farrar and A. J. Stanley
1886—W. Renshaw and E. Renshaw
 C. E. Farrar and A. J. Stanley
1887—P. Bowes-Lyon and H. W. W. Wilberforce
 J. H. Crispe and Barratt Smith
1888—W. Renshaw and E. Renshaw
 P. Bowes-Lyon and H. W. W. Wilberforce
1889—W. Renshaw and E. Renshaw
 E. W. Lewis and G. W. Hillyard
1890—J. Pim and F. O. Stoker
 E. W. Lewis and G. W. Hillyard
1891—W. Baddeley and H. Baddeley
 J. Pim and F. O. Stoker
1892—H. S. Barlow and E. W. Lewis
 W. Baddeley and H. Baddeley
1893—J. Pim and F. O. Stoker
 E. W. Lewis and H. S. Barlow
1894—W. Baddeley and H. Baddeley
 H. S. Barlow and C. H. Martin
1895—W. Baddeley and H. Baddeley
 E. W. Lewis and W. V. Eaves
1896—W. Baddeley and H. Baddeley
 R. F. Doherty and H. A. Nisbet
1897—R. F. Doherty and H. L. Doherty
 W. Baddeley and H. Baddeley
1898—R. F. Doherty and H. L. Doherty
 H. A. Nisbet and C. Hobart
1899—R. F. Doherty and H. L. Doherty
 H. A. Nisbet and C. Hobart
1900—R. F. Doherty and H. L. Doherty
 H. Roper Barrett and H. A. Nisbet
1901—R. F. Doherty and H. L. Doherty
 Dwight Davis and Holcombe Ward
1902—S. H. Smith and F. L. Riseley
 R. F. Doherty and H. L. Doherty
1903—R. F. Doherty and H. L. Doherty
 S. H. Smith and F. L. Riseley
1904—R. F. Doherty and H. L. Doherty
 S. H. Smith and F. L. Riseley
1905—R. F. Doherty and H. L. Doherty
 S. H. Smith and F. L. Riseley
1906—S. H. Smith and F. L. Riseley
 R. F. Doherty and H. L. Doherty
1907—N. E. Brookes and A. F. Wilding
 B. C. Wright and K. Behr
1908—A. F. Wilding and M. J. G. Ritchie
 A. W. Gore and H. Roper Barrett
1909—A. W. Gore and H. Roper Barrett
 S. N. Doust and H. A. Parker
1910—A. F. Wilding and M. J. G. Ritchie
 A. W. Gore and H. Roper Barrett
1911—M. Decugis and A. H. Gobert
 M. J. G. Ritchie and A. F. Wilding
1912—H. Roper Barrett and C. P. Dixon
 M. Decugis and A. H. Gobert

1913—H. Roper Barrett and C. P. Dixon
 F. W. Rahe and H. Kleinschroth
1914—N. E. Brookes and A. F. Wilding
 H. Roper Barrett and C. P. Dixon
1919—R. V. Thomas and P. O'Hara-Wood
 R. Lycett and R. W. Heath
1920—R. N. Williams and C. S. Garland
 A. R. F. Kingscote and J. C. Parke
1921—R. Lycett and M. Woosnam
 F. G. Lowe and A. H. Lowe
†1922—R. Lycett and J. O. Anderson
 G. L. Patterson and P. O'Hara-Wood
1923—R. Lycett and L. A. Godfree
 Count de Gomar and E. Flaquer
1924—F. T. Hunter and V. Richards
 R. N. Williams and W. M. Washburn
1925—J. Borotra and R. Lacoste
 J. Hennessey and R. Casey
1926—H. Cochet and J. Brugnon
 V. Richards and H. Kinsey
1927—F. T. Hunter and W. T. Tilden
 J. Brugnon and H. Cochet
1928—H. Cochet and J. Brugnon
 G. L. Patterson and J. B. Hawkes
1929—W. Allison and J. Van Ryn
 J. C. Gregory and I. G. Collins
1930—W. Allison and J. Van Ryn
 J. H. Doeg and G. M. Lott
1931—G. M. Lott and J. Van Ryn
 H. Cochet and J. Brugnon
1932—J. Borotra and J. Brugnon
 G. P. Hughes and F. J. Perry
1933—J. Borotra and J. Brugnon
 R. Nunoi and J. Satoh
1934—G. M. Lott and L. R. Stoefen
 J. Borotra and J. Brugnon
1935—J. H. Crawford and A. K. Quist
 W. Allison and J. Van Ryn
1936—G. P. Hughes and C. R. D. Tuckey
 C. E. Hare and F. H. D. Wilde
1937—J. D. Budge and G. Mako
 G. P. Hughes and C. R. D. Tuckey
1938—J. D. Budge and G. Mako
 H. Henkel and G. von Metaxa
1939—R. L. Riggs and E. T. Cooke
 C. E. Hare and F. H. D. Wilde
1946—T. Brown and J. Kramer
 G. E. Brown and D. Pails
1947—R. Falkenburg and J. Kramer
 A. J. Mottram and O. W. Sidwell
1948—J. E. Bromwich and F. A. Sedgman
 T. Brown and G. Mulloy
1949—R. Gonzales and F. Parker
 G. Mulloy and F. R. Schroeder
1950—J. E. Bromwich and A. K. Quist
 G. E. Brown and O. W. Sidwell
1951—K. McGregor and F. A. Sedgman
 J. Drobny and E. W. Sturgess
1952—K. McGregor and F. A. Sedgman
 V. Seixas and E. W. Sturgess
1953—L. A. Hoad and K. R. Rosewall
 R. N. Hartwig and M. G. Rose
1954—R. N. Hartwig and M. G. Rose
 V. Seixas and T. Trabert
1955—R. N. Hartwig and L. A. Hoad
 N. A. Fraser and K. R. Rosewall
1956—L. A. Hoad and K. R. Rosewall
 N. Pietrangeli and O. Sirola

1957—G. Mulloy and B. Patty
 N. A. Fraser and L. A. Hoad
1958—S. Davidson and U. Schmidt
 A. J. Cooper and N. A. Fraser
1959—R. Emerson and N. A. Fraser
 R. Laver and R. Mark
1960—R. H. Osuna and R. D. Ralston
 M. G. Davies and R. K. Wilson
1961—R. Emerson and N. A. Fraser
 R. A. J. Hewitt and F. S. Stolle
1962—R. A. J. Hewitt and F. S. Stolle
 B. Jovanovic and N. Pilic
1963—R. H. Osuna and A. Palafox
 J. C. Barclay and P. Darmon
1964—R. A. J. Hewitt and F. S. Stolle
 R. Emerson and K. N. Fletcher
1965—J. D. Newcombe and A. D. Roche
 K. N. Fletcher and R. A. J. Hewitt
1966—K. N. Fletcher and J. D. Newcombe
 W. W. Bowrey and O. K. Davidson
1967—R. A. J. Hewitt and F. D. McMillan
 R. Emerson and K. N. Fletcher
1968—J. D. Newcombe and A. D. Roche
 K. R. Rosewall and F. S. Stolle
1969—J. D. Newcombe and A. D. Roche
 T. S. Okker and M. C. Riessen
1970—J. D. Newcombe and A. D. Roche
 K. R. Rosewall and F. S. Stolle
1971—R. S. Emerson and R. G. Laver
 A. R. Ashe and R. D. Ralston
1972—R. A. J. Hewitt and F. D. McMillan
 S. R. Smith and E. J. van Dillen
1973—J. S. Connors and I. Nastase
 J. R. Cooper and N. A. Fraser
1974—J. D. Newcombe and A. D. Roche
 R. C. Lutz and S. R. Smith
1975—V. Gerulaitis and A. Mayer
 C. Dowdeswell and A. J. Stone
1976—B. E. Gottfried and R. Ramirez
 R. L. Case and G. Masters
1977—R. L. Case and G. Masters
 J. G. Alexander and P. C. Dent
1978—R. A. J. Hewitt and F. D. McMillan
 P. Fleming and J. P. McEnroe
1979—P. Fleming and J. P. McEnroe
 B. E. Gottfried and R. Ramirez
1980—P. McNamara and P. McNamee
 R. C. Lutz and S. R. Smith
1981—P. Fleming and J. P. McEnroe
 R. C. Lutz and S. R. Smith
1982—P. McNamara and P. McNamee
 P. Fleming and J. P. McEnroe
1983—P. Fleming and J. P. McEnroe
 T. E. Gullikson and T. R. Gullikson
1984—P. Fleming and J. P. McEnroe
 P. Cash and P. McNamee
1985—H. P. Guenthardt and B. Taroczy
 P. Cash and J. B. Fitzgerald
1986—J. Nystrom and M. Wilander
 G. Donnelly and P. Fleming
1987—K. Flach and R. Seguso
 S. Casal and E. Sanchez
1988—K. Flach and R. Seguso
 J. B. Fitzgerald and A. Jarryd
1989—J. B. Fitzgerald and A. Jarryd
 R. Leach and J. Pugh

THE CHAMPIONSHIP ROLL

LADIES' SINGLES

1884—Miss M. Watson
Miss Watson
1885—Miss M. Watson
Miss B. Bingley
1886—Miss B. Bingley
Miss M. Watson
1887—Miss L. Dod
Miss B. Bingley
1888—Miss L. Dod
Mrs. G. W. Hillyard
★1889—Mrs G. W. Hillyard
Miss L. Rice
★1890—Miss L. Rice
Miss Jacks
★1891—Miss L. Dod
Mrs. G. W. Hillyard
1892—Miss L. Dod
Mrs. G. W. Hillyard
1893—Miss L. Dod
Mrs. G. W. Hillyard
★1894—Mrs. G. W. Hillyard
Miss Austin
★1895—Miss C. Cooper
Miss Jackson
1896—Miss C. Cooper
Mrs. Pickering
1897—Mrs. G. W. Hillyard
Miss C. Cooper
★1898—Miss C. Cooper
Miss Martin
1899—Mrs. G. W. Hillyard
Miss C. Cooper
1900—Mrs. G. W. Hillyard
Miss C. Cooper
1901—Mrs. A. Sterry
Mrs. G. W. Hillyard
1902—Miss M. E. Robb
Mrs. A. Sterry
★1903—Miss D. K. Douglass
Miss E. W. Thomson
1904—Miss D. K. Douglass
Mrs. A. Sterry
1905—Miss M. Sutton
Miss D. K. Douglass
1906—Miss D. K. Douglass
Miss M. Sutton
1907—Miss M. Sutton
Mrs. Lambert Chambers
★1908—Mrs. A. Sterry
Miss A. M. Morton
★1909—Miss D. P. Boothby
Miss A. M. Morton
1910—Mrs. Lambert Chambers
Miss D. P. Boothby
1911—Mrs. Lambert Chambers
Miss D. P. Boothby
★1912—Mrs. D. R. Larcombe
Mrs. A. Sterry
★1913—Mrs. Lambert Chambers
Mrs. R. J. McNair
1914—Mrs. Lambert Chambers
Mrs. D. R. Larcombe
1919—Mlle. S. Lenglen
Mrs. Lambert Chambers
1920—Mlle S. Lenglen
Mrs. Lambert Chambers
1921—Mlle. S. Lenglen
Miss. E. Ryan
† 1922—Mlle. S. Lenglen
Mrs. Mallory
1923—Mlle. S. Lenglen
Miss K. McKane
1924—Miss K. McKane
Miss H. Wills
1925—Mlle. S. Lenglen
Miss J. Fry
1926—Mrs. L. A. Godfree
Sta. L. de Alvarez
1927—Miss H. Wills
Sta. L. de Alvarez
1928—Miss H. Wills
Sta. L. de Alvarez
1929—Miss H. Wills
Miss H. H. Jacobs
1930—Mrs. F. S. Moody
Miss E. Ryan
★1931—Fraulein C. Aussem
Fraulein H. Krahwinkel
1932—Mrs. F. S. Moody
Miss H. H. Jacobs
1933—Mrs. F. S. Moody
Miss D. E. Round
★1934—Miss D. E. Round
Miss H. H. Jacobs
1935—Mrs. F. S. Moody
Miss H. H. Jacobs
★1936—Miss H. H. Jacobs
Frau. S. Sperling
1937—Miss D. E. Round
Miss J. Jedrzejowska
★1938—Mrs. F. S. Moody
Miss H. H. Jacobs
★1939—Miss A. Marble
Miss K. E. Stammers
★1946—Miss P. Betz
Miss L. Brough
★1947—Miss M. Osborne
Miss D. Hart
1948—Miss L. Brough
Miss D. Hart
1949—Miss L. Brough
Mrs. W. du Pont
1950—Miss L. Brough
Mrs. W. du Pont
1951—Miss D. Hart
Miss S. Fry
1952—Miss M. Connolly
Miss L. Brough
1953—Miss M. Connolly
Miss D. Hart
1954—Miss M. Connolly
Miss L. Brough
★1955—Miss L. Brough
Mrs. J. Fleitz
1956—Miss S. Fry
Miss A. Buxton
★1957—Miss A. Gibson
Miss D. R. Hard
1958—Miss A. Gibson
Miss A. Mortimer
★1959—Miss M. E. Bueno
Miss D. R. Hard
1960—Miss M. E. Bueno
Miss S. Reynolds
★1961—Miss A. Mortimer
Miss C. C. Truman
1962—Mrs. J. R. Susman
Mrs. V. Sukova
★1963—Miss M. Smith
Miss B. J. Moffitt
1964—Miss M. E. Bueno
Miss M. Smith
1965—Miss M. Smith
Miss M. E. Bueno
1966—Mrs. L. W. King
Miss M. E. Bueno
1967—Mrs. L. W. King
Mrs. P. F. Jones
1968—Mrs. L. W. King
Miss J. A. M. Tegart
1969—Mrs. P. F. Jones
Mrs. L. W. King
★1970—Mrs. B. M. Court
Mrs. L. W. King
1971—Miss E. F. Goolagong
Mrs. B. M. Court
1972—Mrs. L. W. King
Miss E. F. Goolagong
1973—Mrs. L. W. King
Miss C. M. Evert
1974—Miss C. M. Evert
Mrs. O. Morozova
1975—Mrs. L. W. King
Mrs. R. Cawley
★1976—Miss C. M. Evert
Mrs. R. Cawley
1977—Miss S. V. Wade
Miss B. F. Stove
1978—Miss M. Navratilova
Miss C. M. Evert
1979—Miss M. Navratilova
Mrs. J. M. Lloyd
1980—Mrs. R. Cawley
Mrs. J. M. Lloyd
1981—Mrs. J. M. Lloyd
Miss H. Mandlikova
1982—Miss M. Navratilova
Mrs. J. M. Lloyd
1983—Miss M. Navratilova
Miss A. Jaeger
1984—Miss M. Navratilova
Mrs. J. M. Lloyd
1985—Miss M. Navratilova
Mrs. J. M. Lloyd
1986—Miss M. Navratilova
Miss H. Mandlikova
1987—Miss M. Navratilova
Miss S. Graf
1988—Miss S. Graf
Miss M. Navratilova
1989—Miss S. Graf
Miss M. Navratilova

LADIES' DOUBLES

1913—Mrs. R. J. McNair and Miss D. P. Boothby
Mrs. A. Sterry and Mrs. Lambert Chambers
1914—Miss E. Ryan and Miss A. M. Morton
Mrs. D. R. Larcombe and Mrs. Hannam
1919—Mlle. S. Lenglen and Miss E. Ryan
Mrs. Lambert Chambers and Mrs. D. R. Larcombe
1920—Mlle. S. Lenglen and Miss E. Ryan
Mrs. Lambert Chambers and Mrs. D. R. Larcombe
1921—Mlle. S. Lenglen and Miss E. Ryan
Mrs. A. E. Beamish and Mrs. Peacock
1922—Mlle. S. Lenglen and Miss E. Ryan
Mrs. A. D. Stocks and Miss K. McKane
1923—Mlle. S. Lenglen and Miss E. Ryan
Miss J. Austin and Miss E. L. Colyer
1924—Mrs. H. Wightman and Miss H. Wills
Mrs. B. C. Covell and Miss K. McKane
1925—Mlle. S. Lenglen and Miss E. Ryan
Mrs. A. V. Bridge and Mrs. C. G. McIlquham
1926—Miss E. Ryan and Miss M. K. Browne
Mrs. L. A. Godfree and Miss E. L. Colyer
1927—Miss H. Wills and Miss E. Ryan
Miss E. L. Heine and Mrs. Peacock
1928—Mrs. Holcroft-Watson and Miss P. Saunders
Miss E. H. Harvey and Miss E. Bennett
1929—Mrs. Holcroft-Watson and Mrs. L. R. C. Michell
Mrs. B. C. Covell and Mrs. D. C. Shepherd-Barron
1930—Mrs. F. S. Moody and Miss E. Ryan
Miss E. Cross and Miss S. Palfrey
1931—Mrs. D. C. Shepherd-Barron and Miss P. E. Mudford
Mlle. D. Metaxa and Mlle. J. Sigart
1932—Mlle. D. Metaxa and Mlle. J. Sigart
Miss E. Ryan and Miss H. H. Jacobs
1933—Mme. R. Mathieu and Miss E. Ryan
Miss F. James and Miss A. M. Yorke
1934—Mme. R. Mathieu and Miss E. Ryan
Mrs. D. Andrus and Mme. Henrotin
1935—Miss F. James and Miss K. E. Stammers
Mme. R. Mathieu and Frau. S. Sperling
1936—Miss F. James and Miss K. E. Stammers
Mrs. S. P. Fabyan and Miss H. H. Jacobs
1937—Mme. R. Mathieu and Miss A. M. Yorke
Mrs. M. R. King and Mrs. J. B. Pittman
1938—Mrs. S. P. Fabyan and Miss A. Marble
Mme. R. Mathieu and Miss A. M. Yorke
1939—Mrs. S. P. Fabyan and Miss A. Marble
Miss H. H. Jacobs and Miss A. M. Yorke
1946—Miss L. Brough and Miss M. Osborne
Miss P. Betz and Miss D. Hart
1947—Miss D. Hart and Mrs. P. C. Todd
Miss L. Brough and Miss M. Osborne
1948—Miss L. Brough and Mrs W. du Pont
Miss D. Hart and Mrs. P. C. Todd
1949—Miss L. Brough and Mrs. W. du Pont
Miss G. Moran and Mrs. P. C. Todd
1950—Miss L. Brough and Mrs. W. du Pont
Miss S. Fry and Miss D. Hart
1951—Miss S. Fry and Miss D. Hart
Miss L. Brough and Mrs. W. du Pont
1952—Miss S. Fry and Miss D. Hart
Miss L. Brough and Miss M. Connolly
1953—Miss S. Fry and Miss D. Hart
Miss M. Connolly and Miss J. Sampson
1954—Miss L. Brough and Mrs. W. du Pont
Miss S. Fry and Miss D. Hart
1955—Miss A. Mortimer and Miss J. A. Shilcock
Miss S. J. Bloomer and Miss P. E. Ward
1956—Miss A. Buxton and Miss A. Gibson
Miss F. Muller and Miss D. G. Seeney
1957—Miss A. Gibson and Miss D. R. Hard
Mrs. K. Hawton and Mrs. T. D. Long
1958—Miss M. E. Bueno and Miss A. Gibson
Mrs. W. du Pont and Miss M. Varner
1959—Miss J. Arth and Miss D. R. Hard
Mrs. J. G. Fleitz and Miss C. C. Truman
1960—Miss M. E. Bueno and Miss D. R. Hard
Miss S. Reynolds and Miss R. Schuurman
1961—Miss K. Hantze and Miss B. J. Moffitt
Miss J. Lehane and Miss M. Smith
1962—Miss B. J. Moffitt and Mrs. J. R. Susman
Mrs. L. E. G. Price and Miss R. Schuurman
1963—Miss M. E. Bueno and Miss D. R. Hard
Miss R. A. Ebbern and Miss M. Smith
1964—Miss M. Smith and Miss L. R. Turner
Miss B. J. Moffitt and Mrs. J. R. Susman
1965—Miss M. E. Bueno and Miss B. J. Moffitt
Miss F. Durr and Miss J. Lieffrig
1966—Miss M. E. Bueno and Miss N. Richey
Miss M. Smith and Miss J. A. M. Tegart
1967—Miss R. Casals and Mrs. L. W. King
Miss M. E. Bueno and Miss N. Richey
1968—Miss R. Casals and Mrs. L. W. King
Miss F. Durr and Mrs. P. F. Jones
1969—Mrs. B. M. Court and Miss J. A. M. Tegart
Miss P. S. A. Hogan and Miss M. Michel
1970—Miss R. Casals and Mrs. L. W. King
Miss F. Durr and Miss S. V. Wade
1971—Miss R. Casals and Mrs. L. W. King
Mrs. B. M. Court and Miss E. F. Goolagong
1972—Mrs. L. W. King and Miss B. F. Stove
Mrs. D. E. Dalton and Miss F. Durr
1973—Miss R. Casals and Mrs. L. W. King
Miss F. Durr and Miss B. F. Stove
1974—Miss E. F. Goolagong and Miss M. Michel
Miss H. F. Gourlay and Miss K. M. Krantzcke
1975—Miss A. K. Kiyomura and Miss K. Sawamatsu
Miss F. Durr and Miss B. F. Stove
1976—Miss C. M. Evert and Miss M. Navratilova
Mrs. L. W. King and Miss B. F. Stove
1977—Mrs. H. F. Gourlay Cawley and Miss J. C. Russell
Miss M. Navratilova and Miss B. F. Stove
1978—Mrs. G. E. Reid and Miss W. M. Turnbull
Miss M. Jausovec and Miss V. Ruzici
1979—Mrs. L. W. King and Miss M. Navratilova
Miss B. F. Stove and Miss W. M. Turnbull
1980—Miss K. Jordan and Miss A. E. Smith
Miss R. Casals and Miss W. M. Turnbull
1981—Miss M. Navratilova and Miss P. H. Shriver
Miss K. Jordan and Miss A. E. Smith
1982—Miss M. Navratilova and Miss P. H. Shriver
Miss K. Jordan and Miss A. E. Smith
1983—Miss M. Navratilova and Miss P. H. Shriver
Miss R. Casals and Miss W. M. Turnbull
1984—Miss M. Navratilova and Miss P. H. Shriver
Miss K. Jordan and Miss A. E. Smith
1985—Miss K. Jordan and Mrs. P. D. Smylie
Miss M. Navratilova and Miss P. H. Shriver
1986—Miss M. Navratilova and Miss P. H. Shriver
Miss H. Mandlikova and Miss W. M. Turnbull
1987—Miss C. Kohde-Kilsch and Miss H. Sukova
Miss B. Nagelsen and Mrs. P. D. Smylie
1988—Miss S. Graf and Miss G. Sabatini
Miss L. Savchenko and Miss N. Zvereva
1989—Miss J. Novotna and Miss H. Sukova
Miss L. Savchenko and Miss N. Zvereva

MAIDEN NAMES OF LADY CHAMPIONS

In the above tables the following have been recorded in both married and single identities.

Mrs. R. Cawley	Miss E. F. Goolagong	*Mrs. G. W. Hillyard*	Miss B. Bingley	*Mrs. L. E. G. Price*	Miss S. Reynolds
Mrs. Lambert Chambers	Miss D. K. Douglass	*Mrs. P. F. Jones*	Miss A. S. Haydon	*Mrs. G. E. Reid*	Miss K. Melville
Mrs. B. M. Court	Miss M. Smith	*Mrs. L. W. King*	Miss B. J. Moffitt	*Mrs. P. D. Smylie*	Miss E. M. Sayers
Mrs. B. C. Covell	Miss P. L. Howkins	*Mrs. M. R. King*	Miss P. E. Mudford	*Frau. S. Sperling*	Fraulein H. Krahwinkel
Mrs. D. E. Dalton	Miss J. A. M. Tegart	*Mrs. D. R. Larcombe*	Miss E. W. Thomson	*Mrs. A. Sterry*	Miss C. Cooper
Mrs. W. du Pont	Miss M. Osborne	*Mrs. J. M. Lloyd*	Miss C. M. Evert	*Mrs. J. R. Susman*	Miss K. Hantze
Mrs. L. A. Godfree	Miss K. McKane	*Mrs. F. S. Moody*	Miss H. Wills		
Mrs. H. F. Gourlay Cawley	Miss H. F. Gourlay	*Mrs. O. Morozova*	Miss O. Morozova		

NOTE.—For the years 1913, 1914 *and* 1919-1923 *inclusive the above records include the "World's Championship on Grass" granted to The Lawn Tennis Association by The International Lawn Tennis Federation. This title was then abolished and commencing in* 1924 *they became The Official Lawn Tennis Championships recognised by The International Lawn Tennis Federation.*

Prior to 1922 *the holders in the Singles Events and Gentlemen's Doubles did not compete in the Championships but met the winners of these events in the Challenge Rounds.*

†Challenge Round abolished: holders subsequently played through. ★*The holder did not defend the title.*

THE CHAMPIONSHIP ROLL

MIXED DOUBLES

1913—Hope Crisp and Mrs. C. O. Tuckey
J. C. Parke and Mrs. D. R. Larcombe
1914—J. C. Parke and Mrs. D. R. Larcombe
A. F. Wilding and Mlle. Broquedis
1919—R. Lycett and Miss E. Ryan
A. D. Prebble and Mrs. Lambert Chambers
1920—G. L. Patterson and Mlle. S. Lenglen
R. Lycett and Miss E. Ryan
1921—R. Lycett and Miss E. Ryan
M. Woosnam and Miss P. L. Howkins
1922—P. O'Hara-Wood and Mlle. S. Lenglen
R. Lycett and Miss E. Ryan
1923—R. Lycett and Miss E. Ryan
L. S. Deane and Mrs. D. C. Shepherd-Barron
1924—J. B. Gilbert and Miss K. McKane
L. A. Godfree and Mrs. D. C. Shepherd-Barron
1925—J. Borotra and Mlle. S. Lenglen
H. L. de Morpurgo and Miss E. Ryan
1926—L. A. Godfree and Mrs. L. A. Godfree
H. Kinsey and Miss M. K. Browne
1927—F. T. Hunter and Miss E. Ryan
L. A. Godfree and Mrs. L. A. Godfree
1928—P. D. B. Spence and Miss E. Ryan
J. Crawford and Miss D. Akhurst
1929—F. T. Hunter and Miss H. Wills
I. G. Collins and Miss J. Fry
1930—J. H. Crawford and Miss E. Ryan
D. Prenn and Fraulein H. Krahwinkel
1931—G. M. Lott and Mrs. L. A. Harper
I. G. Collins and Miss J. C. Ridley
1932—E. Maier and Miss E. Ryan
H. C. Hopman and Mlle. J. Sigart
1933—G. von Cramm and Fraulein H. Krahwinkel
N. G. Farquharson and Miss M. Heeley
1934—R. Miki and Miss D. E. Round
H. W. Austin and Mrs. D. C. Shepherd-Barron
1935—F. J. Perry and Miss D. E. Round
H. C. Hopman and Mrs. H. C. Hopman
1936—F. J. Perry and Miss D. E. Round
J. D. Budge and Mrs. S. P. Fabyan
1937—J. D. Budge and Miss A. Marble
Y. Petra and Mme. R. Mathieu
1938—J. D. Budge and Miss A. Marble
H. Henkel and Mrs. S. P. Fabyan
1939—R. L. Riggs and Miss A. Marble
F. H. D. Wilde and Miss N. B. Brown

1946—T. Brown and Miss L. Brough
G. E. Brown and Miss D. Bundy
1947—J. E. Bromwich and Miss L. Brough
C. F. Long and Mrs. N. M. Bolton
1948—J. E. Bromwich and Miss L. Brough
F. A. Sedgman and Miss D. Hart
1949—E. W. Sturgess and Mrs. S. P. Summers
J. E. Bromwich and Miss L. Brough
1950—E. W. Sturgess and Miss L. Brough
G. E. Brown and Mrs. P. C. Todd
1951—F. A. Sedgman and Miss D. Hart
M. G. Rose and Mrs. N. M. Bolton
1952—F. A. Sedgman and Miss D. Hart
E. Morea and Mrs. T. D. Long
1953—V. Seixas and Miss D. Hart
E. Morea and Miss S. Fry
1954—V. Seixas and Miss D. Hart
K. R. Rosewall and Mrs. W. du Pont
1955—V. Seixas and Miss D. Hart
E. Morea and Miss L. Brough
1956—V. Seixas and Miss S. Fry
G. Mulloy and Miss A. Gibson
1957—M. G. Rose and Miss D. R. Hard
N. A. Fraser and Miss A. Gibson
1958—R. N. Howe and Miss L. Coghlan
K. Nielsen and Miss A. Gibson
1959—R. Laver and Miss D. R. Hard
N. A. Fraser and Miss M. E. Bueno
1960—R. Laver and Miss D. R. Hard
R. N. Howe and Miss M. E. Bueno
1961—F. S. Stolle and Miss L. R. Turner
R. N. Howe and Miss E. Buding
1962—N. A. Fraser and Mrs. W. du Pont
R. D. Ralston and Miss A. S. Haydon
1963—K. N. Fletcher and Miss M. Smith
R. A. J. Hewitt and Miss D. R. Hard
1964—F. S. Stolle and Miss L. R. Turner
K. N. Fletcher and Miss M. Smith
1965—K. N. Fletcher and Miss M. Smith
A. D. Roche and Miss J. A. M. Tegart
1966—K. N. Fletcher and Miss M. Smith
R. D. Ralston and Mrs. L. W. King
1967—O. K. Davidson and Mrs. L. W. King
K. N. Fletcher and Miss M. E. Bueno
1968—K. N. Fletcher and Mrs. B. M. Court
A. Metreveli and Miss O. Morozova

1969—F. S. Stolle and Mrs. P. F. Jones
A. D. Roche and Miss J. A. M. Tegart
1970—I. Nastase and Miss R. Casals
A. Metreveli and Miss O. Morozova
1971—O. K. Davidson and Mrs. L. W. King
M. C. Riessen and Mrs. B. M. Court
1972—I. Nastase and Miss R. Casals
K. G. Warwick and Miss E. F. Goolagong
1973—O. K. Davidson and Mrs. L. W. King
R. Ramirez and Miss J. S. Newberry
1974—O. K. Davidson and Mrs. L. W. King
M. J. Farrell and Miss L. J. Charles
1975—M. C. Riessen and Mrs. B. M. Court
A. J. Stone and Miss B. F. Stove
1976—A. D. Roche and Miss F. Durr
R. L. Stockton and Miss R. Casals
1977—R. A. J. Hewitt and Miss G. R. Stevens
F. D. McMillan and Miss B. F. Stove
1978—F. D. McMillan and Miss B. F. Stove
R. O. Ruffels and Mrs. L. W. King
1979—R. A. J. Hewitt and Miss G. R. Stevens
F. D. McMillan and Miss B. F. Stove
1980—J. R. Austin and Miss T. Austin
M. R. Edmondson and Miss D. L. Fromholtz
1981—F. D. McMillan and Miss B. F. Stove
J. R. Austin and Miss T. Austin
1982—K. Curren and Miss A. E. Smith
J. M. Lloyd and Miss W. M. Turnbull
1983—J. M. Lloyd and Miss W. M. Turnbull
S. Denton and Miss K. Jordan
1984—J. M. Lloyd and Miss W. M. Turnbull
S. Denton and Miss K. Jordan
1985—P. McNamee and Miss M. Navratilova
J. B. Fitzgerald and Mrs. P. D. Smylie
1986—K. Flach and Miss K. Jordan
H. P. Guenthardt and Miss M. Navratilova
1987—M. J. Bates and Miss J. M. Durie
D. Cahill and Miss N. Provis
1988—S. E. Stewart and Miss Z. L. Garrison
K. Jones and Mrs. S. W. Magers
1989—J. Pugh and Miss J. Novotna
M. Kratzmann and Miss J. M. Byrne

THE JUNIORS CHAMPIONSHIP ROLL

BOYS' SINGLES

1948—S. Stockenberg (Sweden)
1949—S. Stockenberg (Sweden)
1950—J. A. T. Horn (G.B.)
1951—J. Kupferburger (S.A.)
1952—R. K. Wilson (G.B.)
1953—W. A. Knight (G.B.)
1954—R. Krishnan (India)
1955—M. P. Hann (G.B.)
1956—R. Holmberg (U.S.A.)
1957—J. I. Tattersall (G.B.)
1958—E. Buchholz (U.S.A.)

1959—T. Lejus (U.S.S.R.)
1960—A. R. Mandelstam (S.A.)
1961—C. E. Graebner (U.S.A.)
1962—S. Matthews (G.B.)
1963—N. Kalogeropoulos (Greece)
1964—I. El Shafei (U.A.R.)
1965—V. Korotkov (U.S.S.R.)
1966—V. Korotkov (U.S.S.R.)
1967—M. Orantes (Spain)
1968—J. G. Alexander (Australia)
1969—B. Bertram (S.A.)

1970—B. Bertram (S.A.)
1971—R. Kreiss (U.S.A.)
1972—B. Borg (Sweden)
1973—W. Martin (U.S.A.)
1974—W. Martin (U.S.A.)
1975—C. J. Lewis (N.Z.)
1976—H. Guenthardt (Switzerland)
1977—V. A. Winitsky (U.S.A.)
1978—I. Lendl (Czechoslovakia)
1979—R. Krishnan (India)
1980—T. Tulasne (France)

1981—M. W. Anger (U.S.A.)
1982—P. Cash (Australia)
1983—S. Edberg (Sweden)
1984—M. Kratzmann (Australia)
1985—L. Lavalle (Mexico)
1986—E. Velez (Mexico)
1987—D. Nargisco (Italy)
1988—N. Pereira (Venezuela)
1989—N. Kulti (Sweden)

BOYS' DOUBLES

1982—P. Cash and J. Frawley
1983—M. Kratzmann and S. Youl
1984—R. Brown and R. Weiss

1985—A. Moreno and J. Yzaga
1986—T. Carbonnell and P. Korda
1987—J. Stoltenberg and T. Woodbridge

1988—J. Stoltenberg and T. Woodbridge
1989—J. Palmer and J. Stark

GIRLS' SINGLES

1948—Miss O. Miskova (Czechoslovakia)
1949—Miss C. Mercelis (Belgium)
1950—Miss L. Cornell (G.B.)
1951—Miss L. Cornell (G.B.)
1952—Miss ten Bosch (Netherlands)
1953—Miss D. Kilian (S.A.)
1954—Miss V. A. Pitt (G.B.)
1955—Miss S. M. Armstrong (G.B.)
1956—Miss A. S. Haydon (G.B.)
1957—Miss M. Arnold (U.S.A.)
1958—Miss S. M. Moore (U.S.A.)

1959—Miss J. Cross (S.A.)
1960—Miss K. Hantze (U.S.A.)
1961—Miss G. Baksheeva (U.S.S.R.)
1962—Miss G. Baksheeva (U.S.S.R.)
1963—Miss D. M. Salfati (France)
1964—Miss P. Bartkowicz (U.S.A.)
1965—Miss O. Morozova (U.S.S.R.)
1966—Miss B. Lindstrom (Finland)
1967—Miss J. Salome (Netherlands)
1968—Miss K. Pigeon (U.S.A.)
1969—Miss K. Sawamatsu (Japan)

1970—Miss S. Walsh (U.S.A.)
1971—Miss M. Kroschina (U.S.S.R.)
1972—Miss I. Kloss (S.A.)
1973—Miss A. Kiyomura (U.S.A.)
1974—Miss M Jausovec (Yugoslavia)
1975—Miss N. Y. Chmyreva (U.S.S.R.)
1976—Miss N. Y. Chmyreva (U.S.S.R.)
1977—Miss L. Antonoplis (U.S.A.)
1978—Miss T. Austin (U.S.A.)
1979—Miss M. L. Piatek (U.S.A.)
1980—Miss D. Freeman (Australia)

1981—Miss Z. Garrison (U.S.A.)
1982—Miss C. Tanvier (France)
1983—Miss P. Paradis (France)
1984—Miss A. N. Croft (G.B.)
1985—Miss A. Holikova (Czechoslovakia)
1986—Miss N. Zvereva (U.S.S.R.)
1987—Miss N. Zvereva (U.S.S.R.)
1988—Miss B. Schultz (Netherlands)
1989—Miss A. Strnadova (Czechoslovakia)

GIRLS' DOUBLES

1982—Miss B. Herr and Miss P. Barg
1983—Miss P. Fendick and Miss P. Hy
1984—Miss C. Kuhlman and Miss S. Rehe

1985—Miss L. Field and Miss J. Thompson
1986—Miss M. Jaggard and Miss L. O'Neill
1987—Miss N. Medvedeva and Miss N. Zvereva

1988—Miss J.-A. Faull and Miss R. McQuillan
1989—Miss J. Capriati and Miss M. McGrath